Challenges, Lessons, and Prospects for Operationalizing Regional Projects in Asia

A WORLD BANK STUDY

Challenges, Lessons, and Prospects for Operationalizing Regional Projects in Asia

Legal and Institutional Aspects

Kishor Uprety

THE WORLD BANK
Washington, D.C.

Contents

Foreword

Over the past two decades, there has been a gradual increase in World Bank lending toward the financing of projects focusing on region-specific, rather than country-specific, goals. These types of projects, commonly referred to as "Regional Projects," have often involved multiple countries, regional organizations, or special-purpose vehicles, as well as specific, overlapping, or integrated themes and scope. If the implementation of most of these projects has involved national government agencies only, many have also relied on multicountry agencies, and some others even on private-sector entities. The scale of this move away from the hitherto dominant state-centric model has been far more rapid than expected in some regions, but the move has also led to difficult, if not disappointing, experiences in some others. Certainly, these projects have had to bear their own share of problems in the context of their design and implementation.

Many of the problems Kishor Uprety describes in this study relate to a lack of awareness about the existing legal instruments among those involved in developing such projects, a lack of clarity in the array of applicable policy instruments, and ambiguity in the legal and institutional systems in our client countries; a mix of problems that needs to be clearly understood to be efficiently managed.

This study, therefore, has attempted to distill, primarily from a legal and institutional perspective, the World Bank experience with regional projects in the past two decades, to assess the difficulties involved in their preparation within the World Bank as well as our client countries, and to look at the way of going forward. In that context, in addition to briefly looking at the policy, practice, and lessons that can be drawn, the study also makes some suggestions on how to move forward on regional operations to ensure that the approach taken and the tools used do not, themselves, become a bottleneck.

Awareness of the myriad problems and contentious matters about projects is important in our legal work. It provides us with the opportunity to improve. But improvement, to be effective, needs to be realistic, doable, and balanced. Therefore, realizing that all projects are unique in nature and need to be developed in full cognizance of the clients' needs as well as their legal and institutional framework, this study is not meant to prescribe or proscribe any actions or measures. Its purpose is to review the experience, compare practices, draw some lessons, and share insights. I hope these lessons and insights as well as the thoughtful analysis will be useful to World Bank task teams and development practitioners outside the Bank working on regional development projects. The author is to be commended for contributing useful knowledge that could make a difference in the design and delivery of these types of operations.

Hassane Cissé
Deputy General Counsel
Knowledge and Research
Legal Vice Presidency
The World Bank

Acknowledgments

I have benefited greatly from inputs of many colleagues and peers, without whose thoughtful observations, suggestions, and encouragement this study would not have seen the day. I am particularly grateful to Melinda Good and Sheila Braka Musiime, Chief Counsels for South Asia and East Asia, respectively, for proposing to lead this initiative as well as for providing comments and, in some cases, countercomments and proposals, which helped me to shape the study and hone the analysis and arguments therein.

I am also extremely grateful to Anthony Toft, for his overall encouragement and support, and to Hassane Cissé, Nicolette K. Dewitt, Sidi Boubacar, Syed Ahmed, Melinda Good, and Siobhan McInerney-Lankford, from the Legal Vice Presidency; Salman Zaheer, Erik Nora, and Sanjay Kathuria, from the South Asia Region; and Colin Bruce, Andrew James Roberts, and Jessica Sloan, from the Africa Region, for peer reviewing the manuscript and providing valuable comments, observation, suggestions, and guidance for improvement.

Further, I am grateful to Julie Rieger, Roch Levesque, Elizabeth Hassan, and Matthew Moorhead for their comments and suggestions; to Marco Nicoli, for his continual strategic guidance throughout the process of this publication; to Laura Lalime-Mowry, Christian Tomas, and Dolie Schein for their assistance in research; and to Liaqat Ali Butt, Lauren Cato, and Meseret Kebede for their logistical assistance in various ways.

Most importantly, I am grateful to those many task team leaders and lawyers who actually worked directly on the different projects that have been used as examples in this study.

Needless to stress that although I wholeheartedly acknowledge the intellectual and strategic guidance, and logistical contributions, so generously provided by all mentioned above, I claim full responsibility for all errors and omissions of the study.

About the Author

A lawyer for 30 years, Kishor Uprety has been with the World Bank's Legal Department for 22 years, where he is currently a Senior Counsel. Through the Bank, he has worked on a number of development issues pertaining to about 30 countries in Asia, Africa, Europe, and the Middle East. He has been a guest speaker at many professional and academic institutions on a number of international law and development-related topics, including the role of third parties in international water treaty making, water law reform, transboundary waters, and legal aspects of operations of international financial organizations. He has also designed training programs on legal aspects of operations for the benefit of World Bank's project managers, and has served on the Editorial Board of the World Bank's Law, Justice, and Development series. He has authored seven books and more than two dozen articles on various issues of development, international, and water law. His books have focused on development and peace; institutional frameworks for legal and judicial training; transit regimes of landlocked states; conflict and cooperation on international rivers; combating corruption; and globalizing justice.

Abbreviations

AC	alternating current
APL	Adaptable Program Lending
ASEAN	Association of Southeast Asian Nations
ATIA	African Trade Insurance Agency
BBGP	Bolivia-Brazil Gas Pipeline
BTC	Baku-Tbilisi-Ceyhan
BTE	Baku-Tbilisi-Erzurum
CASAREM	Central Asia–South Asia Regional Electricity Market
CBI	cross-border initiative
CITES	Convention on International Trade in Endangered Species
CPTC	Cross-border Power Transmission Company
DC	direct current
ESMF	Environmental and Social Management Framework
ESSP	Environmental and Social Policies and Procedures
FTA	free trade area
GEF	Global Environmental Facility
GMS	Greater Mekong Subregion
HVDC	high-voltage direct current
ICT	Information and Communication Technology
IDA	International Development Association
IDO	International Development Organization
IGA	intergovernmental agreement
IL&FS	Infrastructure Leasing and Finance Services Ltd
ITSA	Implementation and Transmission Services Agreement
LMB	Lower Mekong Basin
MIWRM	Mekong Integrated Water Resources Management Project
MOU	memorandum of understanding
MRC	Mekong River Commission
MWRD	Multi-purpose Water Resources Development Project

NASA	National Aeronautics and Space Administration
NBI	Nile Basin Initiative
NEA	Nepal Electricity Authority
NIETTP	Nepal-India Electricity Transmission and Trade Project
OECS	Organisation of Eastern Caribbean States
OMVS	Organisation pour la mise en valeur du fleuve Sénégal (Senegal River Basin Development Authority)
PC	participating country
PGCIL	Power Grid Corporation of India Limited
PTCN	Power Transmission Company of Nepal
RERA	Regional Electricity Regulators Association
RO	regional organization
RSA	Rail Services Agreement
RTFP	Regional Trade Facilitation Project
SAARC	South Asian Association for Regional Cooperation
SAGP	Southern Africa Gas Pipeline
SDF	SAARC Development Fund
SJVNL	Sutlej Jal Vidyut Nigam Ltd
WAGP	West Africa Gas Pipeline Project
WARFP	West Africa Regional Fisheries Program

CHAPTER 1

Introduction

For the past decade and a half, the international development organizations (IDOs) have been making continual efforts to finance multicountry projects with regional goals. Despite their efforts, the structure of intervention through projects with regional development goals has not been easy to design and implement. In particular, difficulties have arisen in the Asian, and specifically in the South Asian, context. Experience shows that one of the reasons has been the lack of clarity in the enabling legal framework and tools, to a large extent within the client countries, and, to a limited extent, also within the development organizations.

A cursory review of a sample of projects in a number of sectors financed by the World Bank and a few other international financing organizations reveals different (if not unique) approaches in the design. These differences can often be attributed to the distinct legal, institutional, and political environments of different countries. In difficult environments, more time had to be spent in the preparation of such projects, thus increasing their opportunity costs.

This study, therefore, is born of a need for more precise and comprehensive information about the legal and institutional aspects involved in designing regional projects. Based essentially on desk study, with limited field consultation, its objective is to share information from places where such projects have been successfully designed and smoothly implemented and to review the general legal and institutional tools, prospects, and opportunities for designing and implementing such projects.

It is important to highlight at the outset that, in spite of some brief introductory discussions in chapter 2, primarily meant for setting the stage, this is not a study about regional integration *per se*, nor the aspects of its delivery, which, understandably, remain a much larger topic, and beyond its scope. It is about "regional projects" in a narrow sense. Moreover, the study has a particular focus on Asia, so as to adapt the features of the successful regional projects and use them, if deemed applicable, in the Asian context. In this vein, this study intends to examine the emerging practice in the different parts of the Bank, in preparing regional projects and to draw lessons. In so doing, it also reviews the framework for regional projects in which international development organizations operate, the problems they face, and the possibilities they provide for countries that rely on international financing for their development.

This study is divided into eight chapters, broadly covering the theory and the practice in different places, and identifying the opportunities and prospects for adaptability in Asia. Following this introduction, chapter 2 briefly touches upon the concept and meaning of a region, the purpose and the value of regionalism, the needs and justifications for preparing regionwide operations, and briefly describes the different types of regional organizations along with their institutional framework. These discussions are followed by narrowing down the scope to a more detailed discussion of regional projects. The definition of regional projects for the purpose of this study is covered in chapter 3. In view of the significance of political will and commitment in all operations of this type (in other words, ownership of countries participating in such projects), chapter 4 devotes a few paragraphs to discuss the value of political commitment of countries and the efforts required to securing it.

Chapter 5 is about the general legal structure applicable to regional projects. In addition to briefly discussing the different scenarios in which the World Bank may be called for intervention, it also reviews, through several subsections, the instruments and implementation modalities that have been used, both the most common ones and the particular and unique ones. The overview is followed by a recapitulation, in a schematic form, of the organizational and decision-making models.

At this juncture, it is important to emphasize that this study does not purport to describe all the regional operations that have been financed so far, but to portray, as examples, the salient features of some selected projects, as relevant from a legal and institutional standpoint only. It does not necessarily aim at addressing the delivery and implementation aspects, except merely in passing, and for the unique purpose of creating a thread to facilitate the understanding of the general trend, and the legal aspects pertaining to these types of operations. Attempts are made, to the extent relevant and practical, to include at least one sample per region, where the World Bank has intervened through financing.

Chapter 6 is about the special and unique situation of Asia, the main focus of this study, and the challenges resulting from its uniqueness. In that context, it touches upon a number of critical legal and institutional elements that are seemingly absent in the Asian context, and which make it difficult to smoothly operationalize regional projects, along with specific difficulties encountered by project teams. Following the discussions of the critical elements that are absent, chapter 7 makes some proposals for consideration, by teams in developing regional projects. However, it should be made clear, this study intends to neither be proscriptive nor prescriptive, in any manner whatsoever.

Finally, the study provides a brief conclusion in chapter 8, followed by a list of selected references, which, the author hopes, will be useful for those who wish to conduct further research on the topic.

CHAPTER 2

General Setting

To be able to appreciate well the notion of "regional projects," it is important to understand broadly the concept of a region, the meaning of regionalism, the purpose and advantages of relying on regional objectives in development, and the different institutional frameworks that exist in the world.

Need for Regionalism

A "Region" is defined as "a broad geographic area containing a population whose members possess sufficient historical, cultural, economic, or social homogeneity to distinguish them from others."[1] "Regionalism," on the other hand, a term commonly used by political scientists, diplomats, and development professionals, is an approach to relations among countries that integrates policy and management specifics to deal with the different issues and concerns pertaining to the region. Regionalism is "integrative" for two main reasons. First, it looks beyond political and jurisdictional boundaries, embracing a distinctly trans-boundary approach that recognizes the natural territory of public issues (such as watersheds, ecosystems, bioregions, or other organic regions).[2] Second, although it may typically start by focusing on a narrow specific issue, a regional initiative, eventually, touches on a mix of broad social, economic, political, environmental, and developmental issues.[3]

Scholars have noted four primary forces converging to justify the need for regionalism. First, regionalism is an organic, inner-directed response (of countries) to human needs and interests.[4] The comparative advantage of regionalism as a framework for policy and management is its insistence on addressing human needs and interests according to the "natural geography" of the problem (or opportunity). This approach has mainly emerged from different scattered attempts to protect endangered species and their habitat, an improved understanding of ecosystems (or "natural regions"), and an increased ability and willingness of the different actors (countries and organizations) to take integrative approaches to solving common problems. Regionalism inherently recognizes the value of integrating social, economic, political, and environmental concerns and multiple competing interests.[5]

Second, advancements in information, communication, and transportation technologies allow people to work together at global, continental, and subcontinental scales. Globalization of the last decade has further led to the integration of the world's economies, which forces people and countries to think and act regionally to remain competitive, both to sustain the local economy and to interact with markets around the globe.[6]

Third, regionalism is, to a certain extent, a response to the failure of existing institutions (social, economic, legal, and political governance, in all forms) to effectively solve problems that transcend political and jurisdictional boundaries. People and countries are now, indeed, looking for better ways to resolve transboundary issues.

Fourth, the emphasis on decentralized (as opposed to centralized) and empowered governments compels nations and communities to think and act regionally to pool resources (to deal with resource scarcity) and resolve common problems. In short, regionalism is proving to be an effective way to sustain development landscapes, and in this context, also represents attempts to preempt heavy-handed or misguided regulatory enforcement in one particular area in one particular country. The larger the playing field, the more resources can be applied to the problem, and the easier it is to make trade-offs among competing interests.[7]

Purpose of Regionalism

Regionalism also serves a number of other "soft" purposes. Knowledge building, thereafter sharing, is perhaps the most important one.[8] Indeed, through regionalism, initiatives can be designed to promote a deeper sense of the social, economic, political, and ecological characteristics of a particular region, or to develop the capacity of citizens and officials within a region to work together on issues of common concern. This knowledge building can become the foundation for more regional initiatives, suggesting that most often it is a necessary condition before moving on to other bigger objectives.

In addition to fostering awareness and understanding of a particular region, initiatives can be expressly designed to stimulate dialogue, mutual understanding, and a common sense of space within a particular region. Councils, committees, groups, or other place-based partnerships, for instance, can start as forums to exchange ideas and better understand the region, and later, can take on other objectives, such as solving particular problems, or working to improve planning and decision-making processes in the region.

Regional initiatives can also be useful to share scarce resources (including information resources) to improve coordination of programs and services among agencies, organizations, and countries within a region, and to provide input and advice in the spirit of solving particular problems. Promoting a distinctive sociopolitical agenda within a particular region, pursuing environmental objectives, promoting economic opportunities, or fostering international planning are some important examples.

Finally regional initiatives can also improve governance, that is improve the making, administration, and enforcement of policy within a designated region. As well as from traditional intergovernmental cooperation, this improvement may come from the mobilization of civil society or the participation of other nonstate actors, which have proliferated in the last decade and have acquired a special status in public international law.[9]

General Institutional Frameworks

Given the diversity of objectives, purposes, and origins the regional initiatives may portray, it is not surprising that there are many different institutional arrangements and models for creating and structuring regional entities. Oftentimes, these institutional models overlap or progress from one type to another. For instance, there are *ad hoc* partnerships, arrangements most often characterized as citizen-driven initiatives, emerging from the efforts of citizens with a common interest in a particular region or a particular theme, and often without any official government sanction or authority, and mostly without the inclusion of a government representative. Similarly, there are nongovernmental organizations, initiatives that are designed to promote common objectives and formed and governed as not-for-profit endeavors. There are also research organizations, oftentimes affiliated with a university or educational institutions whose primary goal is to gather and disseminate mostly technical and specialized information. A number of centers for research, study, and theory development on regional issues, or think tanks, tend to emphasize multidisciplinary approaches to exploring the natural, cultural, legal, political, and economic aspects of decision making and policy making.

On a different platform, there are also initiatives that are government sponsored, or catalyzed, and/or supported by one or more levels of government. Composed of several subcategories, these initiatives may be formed through Statutory Laws (recognized by state legislature); Executive Orders (mandated through executive action); or Interstate/International Compacts (compacts between state or/and agencies or memoranda of understanding, under which various groups attempt to coordinate or mutually delegate some level of planning or authority). In terms of creation, these initiatives may be agency driven (when a state agency realizes that there is a problem or issue that is of public interest, and in response, one or more agencies take the initiative to create an *ad hoc* partnership), or hybrid (including groups that originated under one institutional framework and were later transformed into another type of institution or organization).

Whatever the form may be, these groupings play an important role in shaping regional or group agenda, including agenda for world development.

Regional Groupings for Development

For several decades, regional organizations have been playing a markedly important role in development. These are international organizations, incorporating international membership and encompassing geopolitical entities that operationally transcend a single nation state. Often, their membership is characterized by boundaries and demarcations specific to a defined and unique geography, such as continents; or geopolitics, such as economic blocs; or sectoral specializations, such as agriculture, education, health, or social protection. Most have been established to foster cooperation and political and economic integration or dialogue among states or entities within a restrictive geographical or geopolitical boundary. They reflect both common patterns of development and history that have been fostered mainly since the end of World War II as well as the fragmentation inherent in globalization. However, most regional organizations tend to work alongside well-established multilateral organizations such as the United Nations.[10]

While in many instances regional organizations are simply referred to as international organizations, in many others it makes sense to specifically use the term "regional organizations" to stress the more limited scope of a particular membership. There are hundreds of regional organizations in the world, such as the African Union, European Union, the Organization of American States, the League of Arab States, the Association of Southeast Asian Nations, the South Asian Association for Regional Cooperation, and so forth. Narrowing down the classification, scholars also, oftentimes, refer to continental organizations (that cover the entire geographical area of continent) as opposed to regional organizations (that cover specific geographical areas or a subregion only).[11]

At this juncture, it may also be useful to distinguish cooperation (which does not necessarily focus on process) from integration (which predominantly focuses on process), terms frequently used in modern development parlance. Cooperation may or may not be rooted in distinctive organizations. Although broadly speaking the two concepts overlap, it is only when the regional organization in question acquires some legitimate capacity to act on its own by initiating proposals, making decisions, and implementing policies that the regionalism can be said to switch from cooperation to integration.

Starting from the late 1970s, the world saw an exponential increase in the number of regional groupings, especially at the intergovernmental level, following the example of the European Union. Since then, regional grouping (*regional blocs* or *regional organizations*) in most continents, with varying legal and constituent instruments, has been a vehicle for capitalizing on the benefits of reduced costs, increased cooperation for a peaceful and harmonious neighborhood and, in many cases, development.[12] The purpose of their creation has varied widely: for regional economic development, for trade, for human rights, and so forth, directly or indirectly relevant to development. There are also special-purpose regional organizations, created for carrying out specific sets of activities within the territories of members. For instance, the Organisation pour la mise en valeur du fleuve Senegal, the Eastern Caribbean Telecommunications Authority, the Mekong River Commission, or the African Trade Insurance Agency would fall under this category.

In spite of abundance of entities established for the purpose of carrying out regionally oriented development activities, the International Development

Organizations (IDOs) that are created with the objective of providing funds for development projects to their member countries, in general, still have not been able to adequately focus on projects with broad regional objectives. Nor have they been able to optimize the use of services of sector-focused, subregional or regional entities and organizations, or special-purpose multicountry entities (collectively referred to as ROs), formed in different continents, as a vehicle in the carrying out of the activities, or channeling funds to the targeted areas.[13] These IDOs have been narrowly focusing on taking a country-specific, rather than region-specific, approach to development while funding projects and initiatives from their resources. The reason may be understandable as it relates to history. Indeed, in the past, development was considered largely synonymous with industrialization. Its ultimate goal was fairly clear: to raise incomes and in the process give poor people access to the range of goods and services then widespread in developed societies.[14] Nowadays the concept has widened extensively and development means much more than the tangible goods and services, and requires multiple types and forms of intervention, including interventions through regional or subregional entities.

Notes

1. Webster's Unabridged Third New International Dictionary (3rd ed. 1993). See also, for a very insightful and comparative definition, Arie M. Kacowicz, "Regionalization, Globalization, and Nationalism: Convergent, Divergent, or Overlapping?" Kellogg Institute Working Paper #262 (December 1998), 8–9. See also Antony Anghie, "Identifying Regions in the History of International Law," in *The History of International Law*, ed. Bardo Fassbender et al. (Oxford University Press, 2012), 1058–78.

2. Environmental problems often include externalities that require a larger perspective than that of a single country. A shared vision or joint agreement regarding the priority of various issues and common strategies on how to address them at the regional and country levels is generally needed to facilitate the desired change. Multicountry arrangements require joint action that, if not wanted or considered a priority by a given country, may lead to unwillingness to address the problem by one or more countries. Even under the most favorable circumstances, multicountry arrangements need organizational solutions specially designed for multicountry purposes.

3. In this context, the 1990s witnessed the parallel forces of globalization and regionalization strongly at work. While seemingly contradictory, they are in fact complementary dimensions of market development. See Robert Devlin and Lucio Castro, "Regional Banks and Regionalism: A New Frontier for Development Financing," Paper prepared for a Conference on Financing for Development: Regional Challenges and the Regional Development Banks at the Institute for International Economics (2002), 1.

4. Looking at this broadly from a regional integration angle, it becomes even more relevant. Indeed, regional integration is a complex process, often represented as having three dimensions:
   (1) Hard infrastructure: developing regional transport, energy, and telecommunications networks and setting in place the institutional arrangements for their management and maintenance

(2) Soft infrastructure: removing intangible barriers to the free movement of goods, services, capital, and labor, and creating the institutional frameworks necessary to integrate markets, for example dismantling trade barriers, harmonizing policies to promote intraregional trade and investment, creating institutions to manage trans-boundary markets, and improving the regional business environment

(3) Regional public goods: establishing common arrangements for managing shared resources like water; financing joint investments in agricultural productivity and climate change adaptation; and managing the cross-border dimensions of major health issues, labor migration, and other areas that benefit the region as a whole.
       See for instance, Saoussen Ben Romdhane and Emanuele Santi, "Defining Regional Integration: Key Concepts and Theories," in *Unlocking North Africa's Potential through Regional Integration: Challenges and Opportunities*, ed. Emanuele Santi, Saoussen Ben Romdhane, and William Shaw (AfDB, 2012), 17.

5. Actually Bela Balassa, in 1987, had already distinguished five main types of regional arrangements which involve different trade and welfare effects for regional partners as well as for third countries:

   • A free trade area (FTA) where trade restrictions among member countries are removed in full, while each country retains its own trade policy against third countries. In this case, rules of origin become necessary in order to establish the conditions under which an item qualifies for preferential access within the area. Many FTAs have now included provisions to liberalize investment rules, services trade, and government procurement

   • A customs union which goes one step further than an FTA and adopts a common external tariff against third countries

   • A common market which is a custom union that also allows for the free movement of factors of production (capital and labor) among member countries

   • A monetary union which is a common market with a single currency and monetary policy

   • An economic union which extends the integration process beyond that of a common market by including harmonization of some of member countries' economic policies, particularly macroeconomic and regulatory policies. See Santi et al., *supra* note 4, 16.

6. Regional integration occurs naturally, albeit very unevenly, during the course of the development of private markets. "Natural" market integration is a process characterized by progressive convergence of economic and social parameters between locals and regions and increasing degrees of interdependence. See Devlin and Castro, *supra* note 3, 1.

7. Attempts to harmonize laws in several regions that started a decade and a half ago, for instance, are examples of responses to this phenomenon. The institutional structures among countries aiming at working jointly at a regional level through a multicountry project may vary. Also, establishing a common incentive and enforcement structure for the entire multicountry project may be difficult. Actually multicountry coordination of policy reforms requires mutual trust which often can only be created over a long time span. In this regard, a relatively powerful regional coordinating unit, perhaps backed by a treaty or a convention, has been found to be helpful in supporting the process of political and legislative harmonization.

8. Knowledge systems have been recognized as central to development effectiveness and policy quality, but, as noted by an authoritative report, they remain underappreciated, undersupported, and underused in addressing the central challenges of our globalized era. The situation is even worse in developing countries. See, for example, "Executive

Summary," Networks for Prosperity: Achieving Development Goals through Knowledge Sharing (UNIDO, 2012), 10–11.

9. Even though they do not belong to any established institution of a state, nonstate actors can participate or act in international relations, and as such have sufficient power to influence and cause a change. The admission of nonstate actors into international relations theory goes against the assumptions of internationalists that interactions among states are the main (if not the only) relationships of interest in studying international events. The proliferation of nonstate actors in the post-1990s era and the globalization of recent times have been factors leading to shift in thinking in international politics and law, and to the erosion of power and sovereignty from the traditional Westphalian concept of nation-state. Notwithstanding the ongoing debate between opponents and proponents on their real status, nonstate actors can, however, aid in opinion building in international affairs and formal international organizations should be amenable to using them in their development interventions, particularly as implementing partners. For discussions on nonstate actors, see generally, Philip Alston, ed., *Non State Actors and Human Rights* (Oxford University Press, 2005).

10. Some scholars caution that the distinct trends toward regionalization in the world economy that could be observed in recent years should not be interpreted merely as the formation of economic blocs or "fortresses." This would amount to adopting a biased, backward-looking approach that sees only the somber experiences of the thirties and forties and does not take sufficient account of the different challenges of the postwar period. See for instance, Detlef Lorenz, "Regionalisation versus Regionalism—Problems of Change in the World Economy," *Intereconomics* (January/February 1991), 3; for further discussion, see also Paul F. Diehl, *The Politics of International Organizations. Patterns and Insights* (Dorsey Press, 1989).

11. For general discussions on various types of regional organizations, see Encyclopedia of Public International Law (Section on Regional Cooperation and Organization) (North-Holland 2000). See also for detail on the history of regional organizations, Ruth C. Lawson, *International Regional Organizations. Constitutional Foundations* (Praeger, 1962), v–xiii; see also Dictionary of International Organizations (2008). For a brief discussion of ASEAN and SAARC, see chapter 6, this volume.

12. See Lawson, *supra* note 11; see also Detlef Lorenz, "Regionalisation versus Regionalism," *supra* note 10, 3. See, for some discussion on the modus operandi of IFI, in particular the World Bank, Joan Edelman Spero, "Chapter on the Management of International Economic Relations Since World War II," in *The Politics of International Economic Relations*, 3rd ed. (St Martin Press, 1985), 25–32.

13. For instance, Article V Section 2(c) of the IDA Articles of Agreement provides as follows: "The Association may provide financing to a member, the government of a territory included within the Association's membership, a political subdivision of any of the foregoing, a public or private entity in the territories of a member or members, *or to a public international or regional organization*" (emphasis added). This provision confirms the IDA's mandate to provide financing to public international or regional organizations.

The IBRD Articles, more broadly, state that the Bank may guarantee, participate in, or make loans to any member or any political subdivision thereof and any business, industrial, and agricultural enterprise in the territories of a member, subject to a number of conditions. One of the conditions is that when the member in whose territories the project is located is not itself the borrower, the member or the central bank or some comparable agency of the member which is acceptable to the Bank, has to fully guarantees the repayment of the principal and the payment of interest and other charges on the loan. See Section 4, Article III(i).

14. See John Rapley, *Understanding Development: Theory and Practice in the Third World*, 3rd ed. (Lynne Rienner Publishers, 2008), 1.

CHAPTER 3

World Bank Approach

As highlighted by the former President McNamara, in 1972, "[B]asically the World Bank's operations are shaped by the needs of the development programs of individual developing countries, and the part the Bank can play, with other development agencies, in satisfying those needs."[1] Indeed, for this reason, World Bank-financed activities have usually been examined on a country-by-country basis.

Although a number of development operations (projects, programs, and initiatives) through ROs and/or with regional objectives have been financed in the course of its history, the World Bank's engagement in regional projects can still be considered relatively new.[2] Until the end of the last decade, its engagement was quite limited, less formalized, and often based on *ad hoc*, rather than structured, decision making.[3] Its more formal/institutionalized and structured engagement with such projects began only quite recently[4] and now concerns almost all the development regions, although in some continents such operations are more numerous than in others. This certainly represents an interesting strategic shift that international financing institutions have undergone in recent years particularly dominated by the concern of creating a right balance among development projects, given finite financing envelopes, the need to leverage on multiple levels, the need to deliver optimal outcomes, as well as the political will of countries to give priority to the allocation of financing for regional operations.

Broadly, the World Bank considers regional projects as operations:[5]

1. That involve three or more countries ("Participating Countries" or "PCs"), all of which need to participate for the project's objectives to be achievable (that is, the project would not make sense without the participation of all countries)[6]
2. Whose benefits, either economic or social, spill over country boundaries (that is, that generate significant positive externalities or mitigate negative ones)
3. Where there is clear evidence of country or regional organizational ownership which demonstrates commitment of the majority of PCs

4. That provide a platform for a high level of policy harmonization among countries (this is key to the success of a regional initiative)
5. That are part of a well-developed and broadly supported regional strategy.

Many international financing institutions and international organizations with regional vocation have also taken more or less the same approach in defining regional projects broadly.[7] Some may have chosen to define with a heavier focus on institutional linkages and arrangements, while others may have emphasized sectoral and geographical coverage.

For instance, the African Development Bank, which focuses more on institutional aspects, identifies two broad categories of regional projects, the truly multinational projects and national projects with regional implications. Its Charter recognizes, as regional: (i) loans given to subregional institutions to finance common investment programs; (ii) projects that are physically situated in one or more countries and that involve joint investments undertaken and guaranteed by different countries; (iii) national projects that form part of a subregional investment program; (iv) projects that are situated in one country and use of outputs of goods and services for two or more countries; and (v) projects established in one country with a view to achieving a balanced distribution of investments among countries participating in a subregional integration scheme.[8]

On the other hand, a definition focusing on the thematic aspect is provided by a paper published by the Asian Development Bank. It defines a regional (cross-border or transnational) infrastructure project as a project with activities such as physical construction works and coordinated actions related to policies and procedures, spanning over two or more countries, or a national infrastructure project that has significant cross-border impact. A national infrastructure project has significant cross-border impact if it satisfies one or more of the following criteria: (i) the planning and implementation involves cooperation and coordination between two or more countries; (ii) as per the predetermined plan, produces significant sales of goods or services across regional borders (where significant means at least 20 percent or more of the total sales); and/or (iii) involves the construction of specific infrastructure, such as a road, bridge, or tunnel located on or largely on the territory of a country near the border and is necessary to link the country to the network of a neighboring country or a third country.[9]

Although differing in form, both definitions, in substance, capture the same thought and spirit.

At this juncture, it is important to clarify the distinction between the regional projects and those multicountry initiatives where an umbrella legal framework may exist to define broad objectives but projects are identified and benefits accrue on a country by country basis.[10] As important, multicountry initiatives do not necessarily require concerted action from a group of countries for all potential benefits to accrue to any one country, whereas a regional project does require concerted efforts to be successful and optimal, and benefits accrue on a regional basis. One particular country's unilateral decision can easily affect another country negatively.

Challenges, Lessons, and Prospects for Operationalizing Regional Projects in Asia
http://dx.doi.org/10.1596/978-1-4648-0138-9

It is equally important, at this point, to note that preparing/developing a regional project provides access to additional finance to the borrowing/receiving countries, coming out of the "regional projects" envelope of the World Bank. These funds are incremental to the regular International Development Association (IDA) allocation for a specific country. Thus, a country, through a regional project, can access additional resources.

This is also why, in the context of resource allocation, the World Bank is expected to focus on two additional criteria when prioritizing. First, it should avoid financing primarily national-level investments with resources allocated for regional investments. For specific investments proposed in the context of regional projects, it should try to secure clear external inputs and participation in focusing on the regional concept itself. Second, given the limited availability of resources against the growing demand for regional project financing, especially from the IDA resources, it is expected to ensure that its funds are considered only as a last resort, that is, only after other options have been ruled out.

It is also adequate to note that regional organizations associated with regional projects are also eligible to receive funds directly. For that to happen, in addition to meeting the criteria for IDA regional projects, six prerequisites have to be confirmed:[11]

1. That the recipient is a bona fide regional organization that has the legal status and fiduciary capacity to receive grant funding and the legal authority to carry out the activities financed
2. That the recipient does not meet eligibility requirements to take on an IDA credit
3. That the costs and benefits of the activity to be financed with an IDA grant are not easily allocated to national programs
4. That the activities to be financed with an IDA grant are related to regional infrastructure development, institutional cooperation for economic integration, and coordinated interventions to provide regional public goods
5. That grant cofinancing for the activity is not readily available from other development partners
6. That the regional entity is associated with an IDA-funded regional operation involving some of the participating member states.

Notes

1. *World Bank Operations. Sectoral Programs and Policies*, "Preface" by Robert S. McNamara (Johns Hopkins University Press, 1972), v.
2. Certainly, it depends on how one defines "regional objectives," and, certainly, therefore, one could also argue that the World Bank has been focusing on regional objectives for decades already, as it has always been concerned with membership as a whole. Such regional objectives can also be observed in the World Bank's interventions on projects on international waterways, forests, climate, and so forth. But this paper takes a much

narrower view of "Regional Objective" and focuses on common regional objectives developed by countries on their own to achieve a specific set of outcomes. See also, for a general account of projects in the context of regional integration, *Unlocking Global Opportunities. The Aid for Trade Program and the World Bank Group* (World Bank, 2009; in particular Section 3 on "Supporting Regional Integration," 22–30).

3. However, the topic of cross-border cooperation to achieve regional integration was actually not totally excluded from the agenda of the IDOs. For instance, in the early 1990s, an initiative, cosponsored by the Bank, the IMF, the European Union, and the African Development Bank, a framework of jointly agreed policies that will be taken up by a voluntary subset of countries within existing regional arrangements, such as the Common Market for Eastern and Southern Africa, the Southern Africa Development Community, and the Indian Ocean Commission, was launched. This cross-border initiative (CBI) aimed at channeling the strong aspirations of the PCs for greater economic integration toward a new integration approach based on the promotion of competition and efficiency in the domestic product and factor markets of the PCs with low protection vis-à-vis the third parties. The initiative went beyond tariff reform to include, inter alia, reform of the rules of entry for private investment and facilitation of cross-border flow of goods and persons. Moreover, many actions under the initiative aimed at further integrating the economies into the world economy as this would increase the benefits from regional integration. Thus, in parallel with eliminating tariffs on regional trade, the countries would substantially reduce the tariffs on third-party trade.

   The CBI approach was to facilitate the efficient handling of the regional dimension of adjustment within the overall reform programs of the PCs. The CBI-supported reforms would be incorporated in Bank-funded economic reform programs at the country level and complement the regular dialogue on economic policy reform. In areas such as trade policy and barriers to cross-border activity, the initiative was expected to help broaden the scope and accelerate the time frame for implementation of actions beyond the pace envisaged under the ongoing reform programs. Indeed, this initiative has helped carve a new way of looking at development work, particularly in Africa. See, for details on the initiative, Report re: "Cross-Border Initiative to Promote Private Investment, Trade and Payments in Eastern and Southern Africa and the Indian Ocean" (World Bank, May 15, 1995), 2.

4. See for some discussions, "The Development Potential of Regional Programs an Evaluation of World Bank Support of Multicountry Operations," submitted to the Committee on Development Effectiveness Meeting February 14, 2007, (World Bank, December 19, 2006).

5. Guidelines for Accessing IDA Regional Funding, World Bank; see also "IDA14 Mid-Term Review of the IDA Pilot Program for Regional Projects IDA14," International Development Association Regional Integration Department, Africa Region (November 2006); see also "Pilot Program for Regional Projects," IDA (October 7, 2003).

6. However, if one of the countries is a country in "Fragile State" status, the involvement of only two countries is deemed to be enough. See, "Partnering for Africa's Regional Integration," Progress Report on the Regional Integration Assistance Strategy for Sub-Saharan Africa (World Bank, March 2011b), 22 (note 16).

7. See, for detailed discussions, John W. T. Otieno, "The Experience of the African Development Bank in Financing Regional Integration Projects in Africa," in *Background Papers, The Long-Term Perspective Study of Sub*-Saharan Africa, Vol. 4. *Proceedings of a Workshop on Regional Integration and Cooperation* (World Bank, 1990), 141.

8. Adapted from the Agreement establishing the African Development Bank.

9. Adapted from B. N. Bhattacharyay, "Demand for Regional Infrastructure in Asia and the Pacific: 2010–2020," Background paper prepared for ADB/ADBI Flagship Study, "Infrastructure for a Seamless Asia" (Tokyo: ADBI, 2008).

10. The Malaria Projects or projects dealing with Food Crisis Response are some of the examples.

11. See, Guidelines for Accessing IDA Regional Program Funding in IDA16

CHAPTER 4

Political Will and Commitment

Simply put, political will is the exercise of an abstract feature of sovereign authority to enforce certain acts for the benefit of its intention, usually for the public welfare. It is an unconditional use of political power. Political will is, thus, an important element—a prerequisite—of a good regional project. Such political will and commitment need to be at the highest level, as they are essential for ensuring efficient operation of multicountry institutions and on-the-ground implementation of the actions identified in strategic projects.[1]

In this vein, the presence of a regional agreement, a treaty, or a convention with progressively more specific commitments is highly beneficial.[2] The involvement of relevant existing organizations has also been useful in clearly improving the commitment of stakeholders and facilitating project implementation. Because project actions often fall within the jurisdiction of several ministries, the formation of interministerial committees, among countries, has also helped induce dialogue and communication.[3] It takes serious commitment and effort on the part of Participating Countries (PCs) as well as development institutions (like the World Bank) to get a regional initiative to the point of being ready for financing as a regional project. As alluded to earlier, one of the most important criteria is clear and full ownership of PCs, which is expected upfront. The political will in favor of regional agenda and goals demonstrated under binding legal agreements (regional, multicountry) with other countries would be considered an adequate element evidencing ownership and an important indicator of the likelihood of success of such an initiative.

Political commitment by all concerned parties was key to the realization of a regional project in Western Africa in the area of water resources development.

Indeed, while approving, in 2006, the Senegal River Basin Multi-purpose Water Resources Development Project (MWRD) (box 4.1), implemented with the assistance of Organisation pour la mise en valeur du fleuve Sénégal (Senegal River Basin Development Authority; OMVS),[4] the World Bank was comforted by the fact that the Heads of States of member countries had signed a treaty to include Guinea (a new entrant) in the OMVS. Also, the effectiveness of the said treaty was made an effectiveness condition for the Bank-financed project.[5]

Box 4.1 Senegal River Basin MWRD Project

The Bank approved three IDA credits and one grant in the total amount of US$110 million to support the development of water resources through a MWRD program, in the four riparian countries of the Senegal River Basin. Mali, Mauritania, and Senegal respectively received credits while Guinea received a grant. The MWRD program aimed at funding integrated water resources development activities focusing at the local level to help generate income among rural communities along the river basin, and targeted the development of joint multipurpose activities to foster economic growth and benefit sharing at the local, national and regional levels.

The first phase of the 10 years adaptable program was specifically aimed at building the foundation for long-term development and sustainability of infrastructure, through institutional strengthening, regional planning, and multipurpose uses of the countries' shared water resources. Indeed, less than 25 percent of the basin's hydropower potential (estimated at 1,200 megawatts), was being exploited. The potential for expanding arable land through irrigation from the waters of the Basin was estimated at 320,000 hectares of which less than 32 percent were developed. Therefore, increased water storage and infrastructure, coupled with multipurpose water resources development and management, were crucial to address the growing demand for water and food, and to ensure sustainable growth in the basin area.

The MWRD also aimed at enhancing regional integration among the riparian countries and modernizing OMVS' institutional, legal, and technical framework to better serve the riparian countries.

Source: Adapted from the Project Appraisal Document on three proposed credits in the amount of SDR 21 M to Mali, SDR 22.2 M to Mauritania, SDR 21 M to Senegal, and a grant in the amount of SDR 12.60 M to Guinea for a Senegal River Basin MWRD Project in support of the first phase of the Senegal River Basin MWRD (APL) Program (May 10, 2006).

For that project, the Bank entered into financing agreements with each of the four member countries and one project agreement with OMVS. The proceeds of the International Development Association (IDA) financing were made available to OMVS under separate subsidiary agreements between each of the countries and OMVS.

The OMVS and its national cells assured the overall coordination and supervision of the project on behalf of the four riparian countries. Also interesting is the fact that part of the activities of the project were implemented through performance-based contracts by different executing agencies (the Société d'Aménagement des Terres du Delta in Senegal, the Société Nationale de Développement Rural in Mauritania, the Programme de Développement de l'Irrigation en Aval de Manantali, in Mali, and the Direction Nationale du Génie Rural in Guinea), thus triggering a variety of legal instruments, rights and obligations, in the course of implementation.

Similarly, in the World Bank-financed West Africa Regional Fisheries Program (box 4.2), in addition to a financing agreement with each of the PCs, IDA also entered into a project agreement with the Commission Sous-Régionale des

---

Box 4.2 West Africa Regional Fisheries Program (WARFP)

The WARFP, launched in 2009, is a regional initiative aiming at strengthening the capacity of Cape Verde, Liberia, Senegal, and Sierra Leone to manage targeted fisheries, reduce illegal fishing, and increase local value added to fish products. The program includes four components: (i) good governance and sustainable management of the fisheries, aimed at building the capacity of governments and stakeholders to implement a shared approach to ensure that the marine fish resources are used in a manner that is environmentally sustainable, socially fair, and economically profitable; (ii) reduction of illegal fishing, aimed at deterring illegal activities which threaten the sustainable management of the marine fish resources; (iii) increasing the contribution of the marine fish resources to the local economies and to West Africa and to increase the share of the value-added captured in the region; and (iv) coordination, monitoring and evaluation, and management, aimed at supporting the several countries to implement and monitor the program in the context of the Sub-Regional Fisheries Commission Strategic Action Plan.

The WARFP is to be coordinated at the regional level by a Coordination Unit, housed in Dakar, reporting to a Regional Steering Committee comprising the Fisheries Directors from each of the participating countries.

Source: World Bank Project Portal 2009.

Pêches, a subregional fisheries commission, which was established and operating pursuant to an intergovernmental treaty among Mauritania, Senegal, the Gambia, Guinea-Bissau, Guinea, Cape Verde, and Sierra Leone.[6]

For a Bank-financed telecommunications project, which was part of a larger program in the Caribbean, member countries signed a memorandum of understanding (MOU) with the Organisation of Eastern Caribbean States (OECS) setting out their respective roles and responsibilities regarding the project.[7] Similarly, in the context of a regional trade facilitation project in Africa, PCs created the African Trade Insurance Agency, an autonomous multilateral agency with administrative and financial independence, before the operation was launched.[8]

In order to record their strong country commitment and ownership (political will) for developing a regional power trade market, in 1992, the six Greater Mekong Subregion (GMS) member countries (Cambodia, China, the Lao People's Democratic Republic, Myanmar, Thailand, and Vietnam)[9] established the GMS Power Forum, and later entered into an Intergovernmental Agreement (IGA) on Regional Power Trade which has been ratified by all six countries.[10] Key objectives of the IGA are (i) cost minimization in planning and operation of power provision; (ii) full cost recovery and equitable sharing of benefits of investments; and (iii) provision of reliable and economic electricity to all parties. In parallel, these countries also established a Regional Power Trade Coordination Committee as the high-level body responsible for coordinating and guiding the market's development. These factors (the establishment of the power forum, the signing of the IGA, and the creation of the Coordination Committee) constitute significant potential for electricity and gas trade within the region and justifications for developing regional projects. As such, the World Bank plans to support a regional investment project in Lao PDR and Cambodia referred to as the GMS Regional Electricity Market (REM) Project (box 4.3).

Aimed at strengthening regional cross-border power trading, the World Bank project (in the form of an adaptable program lending—APL) will focus on constructing a transmission link between Cambodia-Vietnam and Cambodia-Lao PDR, a transmission line in Lao PDR, which will eventually become part of the link between Thailand-Lao PDR-Cambodia, and a load dispatch center in Lao PDR to enable it to improve system efficiency and integrate into the regional grid.

In parallel, a feasibility study for a high-voltage transmission link between Vietnam and the China Southern Grid will also be financed. Geographically, the project involves three GMS countries (Cambodia, Lao PDR, and Vietnam). Cambodia is the recipient of power, and Lao PDR and Vietnam are suppliers.[11]

The Bank has also endorsed comfort provided by countries' general political commitment emanating from multiple framework type international

---

Box 4.3 GMS REM Project

The Lao PDR portion includes: (i) a 115 kilovolts transmission system line from Ban Hat substation in Lao to Stung Treng substation in Cambodia, which would involve investments in Lao PDR to complete the 115 kilovolts transmission system for supply of surplus hydropower form the south of Lao PDR to the province of Stung Treng in Cambodia; (ii) a 115 kilovolts transmission system (Xeset substation to Saravan substation) which constitutes a link in the 115 kilovolts transmission system that would interconnect Thailand, Lao PDR, and Cambodia in southern Lao PDR (which are Attapeu substation, Xekong substation, Xeset-I substation, Ban Jianxi substation), Thailand in the west, and Cambodia in the south; (iii) project design and management; (iv) national and/or regional load dispatch centers; (v) Houay Lamphan Gnai Hydropower Project (65 megawatts, 300 gigawatt hours per annum), part of a group of hydropower projects in southern Lao PDR, to be developed and interconnected for export and domestic use; and (vi) technical assistance for collector substation system.

The Cambodia portion includes: (i) a 115 kilovolts transmission system line from Tai Ninh substation in Vietnam to Kampong Cham substation in Cambodia, to facilitate import of power from the South of Vietnam to the Kampong Cham province in Cambodia; (ii) a 115 kilovolts transmission line from Ban Hat substation in Lao PDR to Stung Treng substation in Cambodia, to facilitate import of surplus hydropower from the south of Lao PDR to the province of Stung Treng in Cambodia; (iii) project design and management; and (iv) detailed feasibility study for a hydropower project.

Source: World Bank Project Portal 2011.

instruments. For instance, in the context of the Nepal-India Regional Trade and Transport Project, under which a series of trade and transit facilitation measures are to be carried out in Nepal, the Bank relied on the framework established by a series of bilateral treaties between India and Nepal, which included the treaties dealing with trade, transit, and rail services, amongst the most directly relevant ones, and those dealing with cooperation to control unauthorized trade, double taxation avoidance, investment promotion and protection, and air services (see also box 4.4), among the indirectly relevant ones.

Political commitment becomes even more important and challenging in projects that aim at linking two regions. In the Central Asia-South Asia Regional Electricity Market (CASAREM), a project under preparation aimed at linking

---

Box 4.4 Nepal-India Regional Trade and Transport Project

Three treaties, of direct relevance to the project, mainly govern trade and transit relations between India and Nepal. They include:

Treaty of Trade. The trade relations between the two countries started with the signing of the Treaty of Trade and Commerce in July 1950. After a series of renewals and modifications, this treaty was renewed for the last time in 2009 for seven years. The 2009 changes broadened the list of primary products with duty free access to India, recognized the sanitary and phytosanitary certificates issued by the competent authority of the exporting country if that authority is internationally accredited, adopted a joint mechanism for clearance of perishable goods, established an intergovernmental subcommittee (in addition to an intergovernmental committee already in existence), and agreed to build capacity, within Nepal, on technical standards, quarantine and testing facilities, and human resources.

Treaty of Transit. The current transit regime is governed by the treaty renewed in 2013 for seven years, which, inter alia, confirmed transit rights through each other's territory through mutually agreed routes and modalities.

Rail Services Agreement. A Rail Services Agreement (RSA) was signed in May 2004, to extend cargo train service to the ICD at Birgunj. A Container Corporation, an India-led joint venture, is operating the ICD. The RSA was modified in December 2008 to allow oil/liquid traffic in tank wagons and bilateral break-bulk cargo in flat wagons, and again in 2012, to allow the movement of containerized railway cargo between all Inland Container/Clearance Depots and Integrated Check Posts between Nepal and India through which Nepal is authorized to carry out third country trade (excluding break bulk and open wagons).

In addition to the above, a number of bilateral agreements (for example, the Agreement of Cooperation to Control Unauthorized Trade, the Double Taxation Avoidance Agreement, the Bilateral Investment Promotion and Protection Agreement, and the Air Services Agreement) also are relevant for trade and transit facilitation.

Source: Adapted from Nepal Treaty Series.

Box 4.5 CASA-1000

The CASA-1000 Project, under preparation, when completed, would comprise: (i) a 750 kilometers high-voltage direct current (HVDC) transmission system between Tajikistan and
Pakistan via Afghanistan; (ii) a direct current (DC) to alternate current (AC) converter station in
Kabul to supply Kabul area; (iii) an AC transmission link between the Kyrgyz Republic and
Tajikistan to supply the Kyrgyz electricity to South Asia via Tajikistan; and (iv) the concomitant
institutional and legal framework to enable such electricity trade. The HVDC transmission line
is expected to commence at Sangtuda in Tajikistan and pass through Kunduz, Pul-e-Khumri,
Kabul, and Jalalabad in Afghanistan and terminate in Peshawar in Pakistan. The total length
of the transmission line is estimated at 750 kilometers of which about 16 percent will pass
through Tajikistan, 75 percent through Afghanistan and 9 percent through Pakistan. In addition, a 430 kilometers 500 kilovolts single circuit transmission line is expected to be partially
financed to interconnect the Kyrgyz Republic to Tajikistan.

Source: World Bank Project Portal 2009.

two Central Asian countries with two South Asian countries (thus in two geographical regions), the Bank has relied on an international agreement to ensure
that such commitment exists. CASAREM is a concept for developing electricity
trade among the countries of two regions through a series of investments. The
four countries that agreed to pursue the idea of CASAREM are the Kyrgyz
Republic and Tajikistan in Central Asia (intended exporters) and Afghanistan
and Pakistan in South Asia (intended importers). Other countries could also join
the initiative as the trade expands. CASAREM (box 4.5) aims at facilitating
regional electricity trade between these countries through the establishment of
physical infrastructure and the concomitant institutional and legal framework.

The development of the first phase of CASAREM, which is to establish the
necessary transmission and trading infrastructure and systems to enable a trade
of 1,000 megawatts of electricity between Central Asia and South Asia, is commonly referred to as "CASA-1000."

Ongoing political problems leading to frequent upheavals in some PCs has led
to slow decision making and the preparation of the project has met with a number of difficulties, but is still on track at this time of writing.

At this point, emphasis must be laid on the reality that securing political commitment through agreements is not always easy. Domestic and international
sociopolitical or geopolitical factors may inhibit countries that are in principle in
favor of developing joint initiatives from entering into binding international treaties. Such situations are quite common in South Asia. For that reason, in some
projects developed in South Asia, alternative means and mechanisms had to be
devised to fill in the vacuum created by the absence of a regional legal or treaty
framework (see chapter 5, section 3 for some discussions).

Complex multicountry and multi-implementing agency structures require
careful preparation, which often leads to longer preparation periods and greater

opportunity cost than single-country settings. The process of developing a shared vision and a framework for action among countries sharing, for instance, a transboundary resource, also requires political commitment and public awareness and collaborative spirit. Many approaches and varieties of arrangements can be found through which countries collaborate.[12] In each of the situations, the legal modalities may vary.

Notes

1. Where the only demonstrated political commitment has been the agreement to proceed with an IDO financing the project, such commitments for policy, institutional, and/or legal reforms and investments have been slow to emerge. This conclusion has been valid, as confirmed by a study, also in GEF projects. See also, for instance, Petri Ollila, Juha I. Uitto, Christophe Crepin, and Alfred M. Duda, "Multicountry Project Arrangements," Report of a Thematic Review (September 2000), 2.

2. Indeed, as pointed out by George Delaume, a notable legal scholar, loans are made or contracted for vastly different reasons ranging from purely financial considerations to the pursuit of political goals or the achievement of such objectives as economic development, monetary cooperation, or peace operations in countries beset by international or external strife. See Georges R. Delaume, "Legal Aspects of International Lending and Economic Development Financing" (Parker School of Foreign and Comparative Law, Oceana, 1967), xxi.

3. See Ollila et al., *supra* note 1, 3.

4. The Organisation pour la mise en valeur du fleuve Sénégal (Senegal River Basin Development Authority, commonly referred to as OMVS) was established in 1972 with the mandate of securing countries' economies and reducing the vulnerability of peoples' livelihoods through water resources and energy development. The OMVS structure at the time of project preparation included the three downstream riparian countries (Senegal, Mali, and Mauritania), but not the upstream riparian country (Guinea). As unilateral actions in the basin could place further strain on the limited water resources, all the riparian countries recognized that the inclusion of Guinea in the framework was necessary. By joining OMVS, Guinea was to be fully involved, along with Mali, Mauritania, and Senegal, in OMVS' decision-making processes and would also realize tangible benefits from the joint management of the Basin resources. See the Project Appraisal Document on three proposed credits in the amount of SDR 21 M to Mali, SDR 22.2 M to Mauritania, SDR 21 M to Senegal, and a grant in the amount of SDR 12.60 M to Guinea for a Senegal River Basin MWRD Project in support of the first phase of the Senegal River Basin MWRD (APL) Program (May 10, 2006).

5. The Bank had abstained from financing the first phase in the series of the OMVS Project.

6. See, Convention Portant Création de la Commission Sous-Régionale des Pêches, dated March 29, 1985.

7. See chapter 5, box 5.1.

8. See chapter 5, box 5.5.

9. Note that the Greater Mekong Subregion (GMS) is not a geological or geographical region, but rather, was a project originally developed by the Asian Development Bank

in 1992 that brought together the six states of the Mekong River basin, namely Cambodia, China, Lao PDR, Myanmar, Thailand, and Vietnam. The term GMS now is being commonly used to refer to the six countries as a group.

10. Inter-Governmental Agreement on Regional Power Trade in the Greater Mekong Sub-Region, 2003. See, International Experience with Cross-border Power Trading, Report to the Regional Electricity Regulators' Association (RERA) and the World Bank (Castalia Strategic Advisors, September 2009), 73; see also generally, Won-Cheol Yun and Zhong Xiang Zhang, "Electric Power Grid. Interconnection in Northeast Asia," East-West Center Working Paper No 63 (March 2005), 1–2.

11. World Bank Project Portal (2011).

12. The collaboration may be based on a "Vision." A Vision is a shared set of objectives and the principles of future actions that benefit all countries willing to participate, but without any binding provisions. By establishing common objectives, a vision statement acts as an initial step forward getting agreement for joint management. It may also be based on an MOU, a document, formal or informal, that records agreed actions, most likely including provisions for resource mobilization, without taking on the binding nature of a treaty. It can further also be based on agreements for joint management of activities for achieving mutually shared goals, or even a convention (a treaty). The essential objective is to create trust, an important ingredient in the success of an operation. Trust is extremely important to meet transboundary objectives. It is built on the back of effective communications, a common set of data, and analysis protocols and transparent decision making across boundaries. For a brief discussion, see also World Bank, "Lessons for Managing Lake Basins for Sustainable Use," Report No. 32877 (Environment Department, 2005), 42–43.

CHAPTER 5

General Legal Structures
for Regional Projects

A regional project can be implemented with the assistance of a regional organization (RO),[1] or without it directly through the Participating Countries (PCs). Implementation modalities can vary enormously. Contingent upon the modalities for implementation, the legal structures for World Bank financing of individual regional projects (or programs) may also vary. The models vary depending on the country situation, the nature and objective of the project, the regional geopolitical sensitivities, the region's legal framework (and its project friendliness), the benefits (private versus public goods), the enforceability (of legal provisions), and a number of other factors. The choice of the structure will depend on issues raised by (i) the Bank's policy framework, (ii) the PCs' own legal frameworks (including any international agreements), (iii) the RO's legal status (if relevant), (iv) the scope and the nature of the project, and (v) practical design decisions ("implementability").[2]

Indeed, as noted by George Delaume, from a legal perspective, analyzing the factors such as the scope and nature of international investment and trade and new institutions (thus their legal relations) is complicated as it involves not only an examination of legal practice and problems on three different levels—the municipal, the international, and the comparative—but also of the effect which it has on the other.[3]

Possible Scenarios

For the purposes of this study and for simplifying understanding, one could roughly categorize the possible legal structures into two main scenarios.

When ROs Are Involved

If funding from International Development Organizations (IDA) resources is directly provided to an RO, a special authorization from IDA's board of executive directors may be required since IDA can only provide funds from additional resources if expressly authorized to do so.[4] On the other hand, if a loan (International Bank for Reconstruction and Development (IBRD) resources) is provided to an RO, then the member countries' guarantee will need to be secured.[5]

With regard to legal arrangements for operations financed by the World Bank, when an RO is involved, unless a special circumstance so requires, generally there would be: (i) one project agreement between the World Bank (IBRD or IDA) and the RO; separate financing (if IDA) or loan (if IBRD) agreement between the Bank and the PCs; and an implementation agreement between the PCs and the RO (figures 5.1a and 5.1b); (ii) one financing or loan agreement

Figure 5.1 Some Simplified Models when Regional Organizations Are Involved

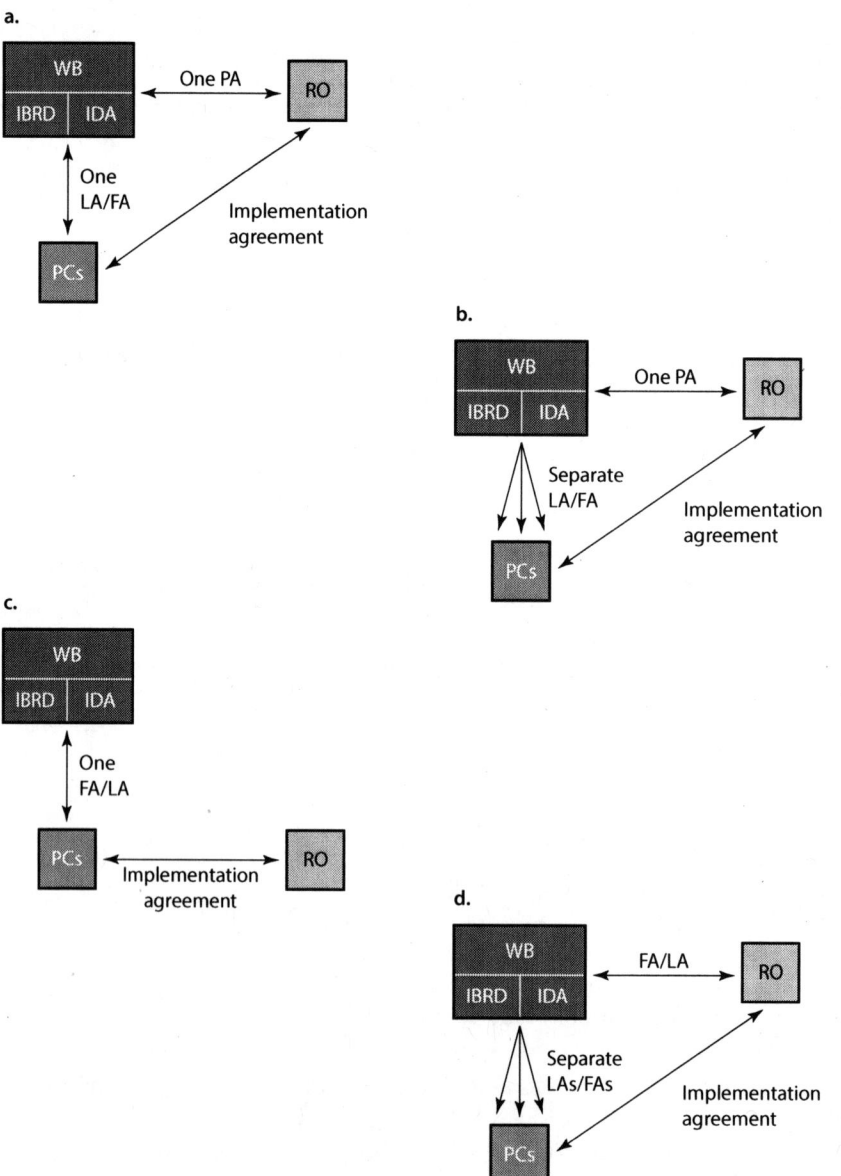

between the World Bank and each of the PCs; and an implementation agreement between the PCs and the RO (figure 5.1c); or (iii) one financing or loan agreement between the Bank and the RO; required numbers of financing or loan agreements between the Bank and the PCs; and an implementation agreement between the PCs and the RO (figure 5.1d). These models may also overlap in many circumstances.

In the case of an IDA Grant, everything else will be the same as above, but, as confirmable by World Bank practice (largely in Africa), instead of an agreement with the PC, a consent letter/endorsement from each one will be deemed sufficient.[6] Also, as a matter of practice, and influenced by the need for prudent implementation, the signing of the implementation agreement between the PCs and the RO has often been included, in the projects' legal documents, as a condition of effectiveness of the whole operation.

As noted in chapter 3 already, several criteria need to be met for an RO to qualify for a grant (as a recipient) under the IDA regional window, including one criteria on "legal personality" under which it should be demonstrated that "the Recipient is a *bona fide* regional organization that has the legal status and fiduciary capacity to receive grant funding and the legal authority to carry out the activities financed."

In assessing whether an RO meets this criterion, it will be important to refer to the constituent instrument of the institution. As regards public international law, such personality may derive from the member states' (the parties to the constituent instrument) delegated power, vesting in the RO the competence required to enable those functions to be effectively discharged, and entrusting such functions to the RO, with the attendant duties and responsibilities. This reasoning was, it may be recalled, also used by the International Court of Justice in 1949, regarding the United Nations.[7] Furthermore the test should investigate the different organs with specific attributions and their relevance to the project in question. Often a declarative resolution, a paragraph in the preamble, or a provision in the body of the constituent instrument would provide for the capacity of the institution: (i) to enter into contracts; (ii) to acquire and dispose of movable or immovable property; and (iii) to petition and be sued in a court of law.

The attributes of legal personality as well as the institution's capacity to receive funding and to execute the project should be clear.

When ROs Are Absent

Unlike the above modalities, in a regional project without the involvement of an RO as well as the legal and institutional antecedents and peripherals associated with it, the legal architecture will have to be modified. Because of the absence of an RO, agreements will have to be with PCs but mechanisms to adequately ensure and reflect the spirit of regionalism will have to be devised.[8] This can often be a challenge as nationalism of independent nations can vary enormously,[9] and can impact the design of such mechanisms.

Challenges, Lessons, and Prospects for Operationalizing Regional Projects in Asia
http://dx.doi.org/10.1596/978-1-4648-0138-9

Instruments and Implementation Modalities: Standard Examples

There is a continuum of sorts, a range of options to be considered when designing the legal architecture for a specific project dealing with more than one country in a region or in multiple regions. The situation and the context tend to dictate the type of legal arrangements.[10] In the Bank, several options have been, and can be, tried. These may include (a) a separate lending instrument with each PC; (b) a single lending instrument with all PCs; or (c) a single lending instrument with an RO.

Separate Lending Instrument with Each Participating Country

In this most common legal structure for regional projects, the Bank enters into a separate loan or financing agreement with each PC. It may also enter into a financing agreement with the RO involved, if the latter will be receiving funds directly from the Bank for the project, or it may enter into a project agreement with the RO if funds will be made available by the PCs to the RO.

The Bank may also require an implementation agreement among PCs that defines their joint and respective responsibilities under the regional program, or it may rely on an existing treaty among them if it covers the elements required by the Bank.

For instance, in the Organisation of Eastern Caribbean States (OECS) telecommunications reform project, the Bank entered into separate IBRD loan and/or IDA credit agreements with the five member states (Commonwealth of Dominica, Grenada, St. Kitts and Nevis, St. Lucia, and St. Vincent and the Grenadines), and a project agreement with the OECS (the implementing RO), which assumed all obligations pertaining to the implementation of the project (box 5.1).

Although an existing treaty establishing the OECS governs the relations among the member states, the member countries signed a single memorandum of understanding (MOU) with the OECS setting out their respective roles and responsibilities regarding the regional program.[11]

Box 5.1 OECS Telecommunications Reform Project

In 1998, five members of the Organisation of Eastern Caribbean States—Dominica, St. Kitts and Nevis, Grenada, St. Lucia, and St. Vincent and the Grenadines—agreed to establish a common regulatory framework for the telecommunication sector. The 1998 agreement committed the five governments to implement a wide-ranging telecommunications reform agenda including a procompetitive legal and regulatory environment, harmonization of laws, negotiations with the incumbent monopoly provider to terminate exclusive agreements, and the establishment of a regional regulatory body. Fulfilling this last obligation, in 2000, they created the Eastern Caribbean Telecommunications Authority (the first regional telecommunications regulatory authority in the world) to facilitate the harmonization of the regulatory regime, under the World Bank-financed project.

Source: Telecommunication Reform in the OECS: Impacts on Prices and Services. A joint Report of the Eastern Caribbean Telecommunications Authority and the World Bank.

Another variation of this model can also be found in East Asia in the context of a Bank-financed water management project involving the Mekong River. The Mekong Integrated Water Resources Management Project (MIWRM) involved an international regional organization, the Mekong River Commission (MRC) (box 5.2).

Designed as a horizontal Adaptable Program Lending (APL), the MIWRM is being financed by two separate grants by the World Bank. A grant in an amount equivalent to US$18 million to the Lao People's Democratic Republic (Lao PDR), and another grant in an amount equivalent to US$8 million to the MRC.

Consequently, the Bank entered into a financing agreement with Lao PDR and another financing agreement with the MRC to carry out the activities within the MRC's mandate.[12] It is expected that Cambodia will join the project as a recipient of Bank financing, at which point another agreement between the Bank and Cambodia may be required.

Another example of a regional project in the water sector comes from the Middle East and North Africa region. A multicountry APL financed by a Global Environmental Facility Grant (GEF Grant), it focuses on the technical assistance and hardware and software infrastructure required to build the capacity of local governments to improve local and regional water resources and agricultural management using earth observation tools.

Box 5.2 Mekong Integrated Water Resources Management (MIWRM)

The objective of the MIWRM project, including three main components, is to establish key examples of integrated water resource management practices in the Lower Mekong Basin (LMB) at the regional, national, and subnational levels, and to contribute to more sustainable river basin development in the Lower Mekong.

The first component of the project focuses on regional water resources management, aimed at increasing dialogue, cooperation, and understanding on MIWRM principles among the LMB countries and supporting: (i) transboundary dialogue; (ii) establishment of an approach for environment impact risk and disaster risk assessment; (iii) communications outreach; and (iv) project monitoring, administrative support, and oversight.

The second component focuses on national water resources management, which aims at strengthening legal, institutional, and human resources to implement MIWRM and improving water resources planning in Lao PDR, and supporting: (i) development of a Water Resources Law; and (ii) institutional capacity building for water quality monitoring, hydrometeorological modeling, and collection and analysis of the hydrometeorological information.

The third component focuses on improved floodplain and aquatic resources management in regionally significant areas, including sustainable community fisheries comanagement in key spawning and feeding habitats of regional significance. This component also supports: (i) river basin and floodplain management in the Xebangfai and Xebanghieng river basins; and (ii) aquatic resources and fisheries management for Lao PDR.

Source: World Bank Project Portal 2012.

Phase 1 of the operation will support activities in Lebanon, Jordan, Morocco, the Arab Water Council, and the Centre Regional de Télédétection des Etats d'Afrique du Nord in Tunisia. Phase 2 will support the same activities in the Arab Republic of Egypt. Each phase comprise three main components: (i) improved water resources and agricultural management; (ii) capacity building and project management; and (iii) regional integration and cooperation.[13]

The GEF Grant from the Sustainable Mediterranean Program (designed along the guidelines of a horizontal APL) in the amount of US$5.644 million, is divided into six individual grants, for which the Bank signed separate grant agreements with each of the beneficiary PCs and a grant agreement with the Arab Water Council (a multicountry entity), which will provide regional coordination function under the program.[14]

Another regional operation, an example from the East Asia region, the Pacific Regional Connectivity Program, is aimed at reducing the cost and increasing the availability of international bandwidth for participating countries, and thereby facilitating the development of a wide range of Information and Communication Technology (ICT) applications to support social and economic development in the Pacific region.

Designed to be implemented in five phases in five different island countries scattered throughout the Pacific Ocean, the total estimated cost of the Regional Connectivity Program is US$186.5 million, with an IDA contribution of US$88.2 million.

The project, jointly cofinanced with the ADB and the Pacific Region Infrastructure Facility, consists of the construction of a landing station and submarine cable starting in a landing station in Tonga and finishing in a landing station in Fiji, and technical assistance to improve the policy, legal, and regulatory framework for telecommunications, Internet, and e-transactions, and overall project management.

As proposed, Phase 1 concerns Tonga-Fiji Connectivity Project (fiscal 2012); Phase 2 concerns Solomon Islands Connectivity Project (fiscal 2013); Phase 3 concerns Samoa Connectivity Project (fiscal 2013/14); Phase 4 concerns Vanuatu Connectivity Project (fiscal 2013/14); and Phase 5 concerns Northern Pacific Connectivity (fiscal 2015). In the first phase, the Tonga-Fiji Connectivity Project was presented to the IDA Board along with a description of the overall program with funds to be made available to other countries as and when they express demand and demonstrate readiness to participate in the program (box 5.3).

Single Lending Instrument with All PCs

The Bank may also take an approach of entering into one single financing agreement with all PCs, setting out both the terms and conditions of the financing, and the respective roles and responsibilities of PCs among themselves and in relation to the Bank. Though simple in appearance and form, this structure can be complicated since it would normally require all PCs to ratify the agreement (in accordance with their respective constitutions and laws) before such agreement becomes effective and the Bank starts to disburse funds. Thus, this model has a

---

Box 5.3 Tonga-Fiji Connectivity Project Implementation Arrangements

The objective of the first-phase project is to improve the enabling environment for telecommunications and ICT in the Kingdom of Tonga, including greater competition and increased access to infrastructure and services by reducing the costs of international connectivity and strengthening the regulatory framework. Tonga has been allocated US$17.2 million equivalent IDA grant (composed of regional and individual country allocations). The Tonga Cable Limited (TCL), to which funds have been passed on under a subsidiary agreement, is implementing the project.

In addition to the standard effectiveness conditions (the signing and effectiveness of the ADB Loan agreement and the Pacific Region Infrastructure Facility Grant agreement, and the signing of the subsidiary agreement), two conditions of disbursements for infrastructure investments are also included:

1. The issuance of the nonexclusive TCL License (with provisions authorizing TCL to: (i) roll out undersea cable infrastructure, including building a cable landing station; and (ii) provide wholesale services (capacity) to holders of valid individual licenses)

2. The signing of a Landing Party agreement between TCL and FINTEL (a limited company established and operating in Fiji), and setting forth FINTEL's obligation to provide "turnkey" services for TCL, including the physical connection to the Southern Cross Cable Network, and obtaining all necessary permits or authorizations on behalf of TCL that it might need to land its cable in Suva.

Source: World Bank Project Appraisal Document for Regional APL for a Pacific Regional Connectivity Program 2011.

---

potential risk of delaying implementation of activities in countries that ratify the agreement but cannot receive any funds, because other PCs have not ratified the agreement yet.

The West Africa HIV/AIDS and transport project is a pragmatic variant of this structure (box 5.4). It aims to enhance access to HIV/AIDS prevention, treatment, and care and support services for high-risk groups and improve the flow of commercial and passenger traffic along the major Abidjan-Lagos Transport Corridor that crosses five West African States. The Bank entered into a financing agreement with a single PC (Benin), which received the IDA grant on behalf of the other participating states.

Each of the other four PCs set out its respective responsibilities in the program, in a unilateral commitment letter to the Bank, pending the ratification by the five member countries of a Convention establishing the Abidjan-Lagos Corridor Organization.[15]

Single Lending Instrument with a Regional Organization

The Bank may also take the approach of entering into a financing agreement directly with a regional organization. Under this scenario, it may require a guarantee from each of the PCs, which sets out their respective roles and

Challenges, Lessons, and Prospects for Operationalizing Regional Projects in Asia
http://dx.doi.org/10.1596/978-1-4648-0138-9

Box 5.4 West Africa HIV/AIDS and Transport Project

In November 2002, representatives of Nigeria, Benin, Togo, Ghana, and Côte d'Ivoire agreed to establish an Abidjan-Lagos Corridor Organization (ALCO) to combat HIV/AIDS. The text of a treaty was agreed and subjected to ratification. On ratification, ALCO, with a legal personality, was to assume all responsibilities for implementing the project (see below) and, upon its completion, for continued operations of ALCO. In the intervening period, Benin agreed to assume responsibility for project implementation, and thus became the designated recipient of the IDA grant in support of the project.

Five key institutional arrangements were made for the duration of the project: (i) a governing body (GB) with the participation of the heads of national HIV/AIDS programs and the ministries of transport in each country; (ii) an executive secretariat of the GB to coordinate and facilitate project implementation; (iii) an intercountry committee to advise the GB on policy and implementation issues; (iv) involvement of sector implementing agencies; and (v) adoption of operational directives.

The ultimate responsibility for the project rests with the GB, composed of representatives of all the five countries. The heads of state of these countries, through a joint declaration, vested the GB with the responsibility for liaising with each member country's respective national programs, and for: (i) the adoption of the work program and approval of annual plans; (ii) the preparation and execution of the multicountry transport corridor strategy and plan of action; and (iii) the review of progress on implementation. To ensure ownership and shared responsibilities, the five countries agreed that Nigeria would hold the presidency of the GB, Ghana would hold the vice presidency, while Benin would host the executive secretariat with the executive secretary being a national of Côte d'Ivoire (to be located at the secretariat in Benin) and that Togo would chair the Inter-Country Advisory Committee.

Source: Project Appraisal Document on a Proposed Grant in the Amount of SDR 12.20 Million to Benin on Behalf of Five Western African States for HIV/AIDs Project for Abidjan—Lagos Transport Corridor in Support of the Second Phase of the Multi-Country HIV/AIDs Program for the Africa Region (September 29, 2003).

---

responsibilities in relation to the Bank, including their guarantee of the financing of the RO. PCs may then enter into an implementation agreement with the RO that sets out their individual and joint responsibilities with respect to the regional program.

In a variant of this approach, in the Africa regional trade facilitation project, which aimed at providing political risk insurance and enhancing access to financing for cross-border trade, the Bank entered into an agreement with the African Trade Insurance Agency (ATIA) to provide a technical assistance credit to the regional organization (box 5.5). It also entered into separate credit agreements with each of the seven member countries, providing a credit to each of them. These seven countries, in turn, signed an implementation agreement with ATIA, detailing the parties' obligations.[16]

An approach similar to the one above was also followed in the context of the Nile Transboundary Environmental Action Project, under which a grant

---

Box 5.5 Africa Regional Trade Facilitation Project (RTFP)

To implement the project, the PCs created the African Trade Insurance Agency (ATIA), an autonomous multilateral body enjoying administrative and financial independence. At the COMESA Summit, on May 18, 2000, the agreement Establishing the ATIA was adopted by the heads of states and recommended for signature. Burundi, Kenya, and Uganda signed the agreement at the Summit, and Malawi, Rwanda, and Zambia signed later. After these six countries ratified the agreement and paid their initial capital contribution to ATIA, the agreement came into effect on January 20, 2001. The secretary general of the Organization of African Unity is the depositary of the agreement, which responsibility has been delegated to the secretary general of COMESA.

ATIA's board of directors, at all times, will have 50 percent private sector representation, and ATIA will manage the facility accordance with an Operations Manual, which spells out the criteria for determining the eligibility of applications, the form of insurance contracts, and the procedures for issuing insurance policies, agreed at negotiations between the respective governments, IDA, and the private insurers.

IDA extended a credit to each country participating in the RTFP. The size of the IDA credit depended on the expected demand for insurance and the size of the economy of each country, and to serve as financial backup to each insurance policy.

Source: Project Appraisal Document on Proposed Credits in the Amount of SDR 85.2 Million to Burundi, Kenya, Malawi, Rwanda, Tanzania, Uganda, Zambia and the African Trade Insurance Agency for a Regional Trade Facilitation Project (World Bank, March 12, 2001).

(US$8 million) from GEF was provided to the Nile Basin Initiative (NBI),[17] an entity executing the project. A single grant agreement was signed with the NBI with a letter from each of the member countries' ministers of finance confirming their respective country's agreement for the NBI to execute the project on their behalf.[18]

One additional point that may be flagged in connection with the instrumentation is the standard requirement, under the World Bank Articles, for a report or a recommendation of the statutory committee for all loans, credits, and grants.[19] However, the procedure followed in connection with the legal requirement of a statutory committee report applies differently to loans or grants made directly to ROs. This key difference in the requirements is noteworthy.

Instruments and Implementation Modalities: Particular Examples

There are some particular examples in Asia that are worth discussing. The particularity emanates from the uniqueness of the region in a variety of ways, and among others, pertains to demand versus supply of goods, capacity, and resources, and the legal, institutional and political environment.

Design Particularities due to Regional Uniqueness

Energy, for instance, seems to be one of the sectors that has great potential for regional projects. Also, interestingly, in this sector, the region consists of both resource surplus and deficient countries, which has interesting ramifications for intraregional cooperation. Nepal, Bhutan, Myanmar, and Lao PDR, for instance, are energy-surplus countries that have the potential to supply clean hydropower or natural gas to energy-deficient countries in the region, like Bangladesh, India, Pakistan, Thailand, and Vietnam. Additionally, Central Asian countries have the potential to supply gas and oil through pipelines to India, Pakistan, and China to feed these countries' growing demands. Cooperation in planning and implementing regional infrastructure projects to share these scarce resources for achieving energy and water security seems almost natural for the region.[20]

A detailed taxonomical investigation of projects (supported by a variety of IDOs) shows that infrastructure has been the sector which is most suited for regional projects. Infrastructure does play a key role in promoting and sustaining rapid economic growth.[21] When properly developed, it can also make growth more inclusive by sharing its benefits with poorer groups and communities, especially by connecting remote areas and small as well as landlocked countries to major business centers and markets, enhancing competitiveness and productivity.[22] Studies have further confirmed that regional trade in energy can take advantage of economies of scale and help countries develop and gain access to low-cost energy.[23] This would be helpful under all circumstances and particularly for small economies.[24]

In East Asia, the demand-versus-supply situation is tricky. The six Greater Mekong Subregion (GMS) member countries are characterized by uneven electricity demand along with mismatched availability of resources for power production. China, Thailand, and Vietnam present fast-growing needs for electric power due to their strong macroeconomic growth. Conversely, Cambodia, Lao PDR, and Myanmar offer an unexploited potential for hydropower supply that, due to the required economies of scale and low levels of in-country electricity demand, cannot be developed economically for domestic consumption. Power trading in the GMS presents great opportunities to develop resources in countries with low electrification rates, for export to countries where electrification rates are higher. However, the number of regional projects under consideration in East Asia is not commensurate with the region's huge potential. Only a few are being developed and, for those too, the pace of advancement is relatively slow.

In South Asia, the energy resource endowments and energy consumption needs among countries are even more pronounced. For instance, Nepal and Bhutan have hydropower potential far in excess of their domestic needs, and Bangladesh has substantial resource of natural gas that could be developed for export either as fuel or electric power, while both India and Pakistan provide major electricity and gas markets. By virtue of its size and population (over 1.4 billion people, more than one-fifth of the world's population), South Asia is, itself, an important world market, which continues to experience rapid growth in energy demand.[25]

The political economy of South Asia[26] makes it a unique case. Conflict has ravaged Afghanistan for decades, India and Pakistan possess nuclear weapons, and the civil conflict in Nepal and Sri Lanka left a serious negative imprint on the society.[27] Much of the violence, as confirmed by reports, stems from South Asia's inequalities and the extremely uneven distribution of wealth.[28] Yet, the region projects an unprecedented potential for transforming its economic and social conditions and playing a key role in the global economy.[29]

All sectors of development are ailing and need curing. From the perspective of regional projects, the greatest potential for development-intervention appears to be in the infrastructure sector, along with subsectors such as power and energy, water management, conservation, trade, transport (including transit facilities), and telecommunication. The most significant and pressing issue currently facing South Asian nations is, as already highlighted, the rapidly rising energy demand and the need to promote cross-border trading to meet it.

But developing regional projects among the South Asian countries, where political suspicions continue and sovereignty concerns dominate discussion of relations, is not easy. A number of conditions will need to be fulfilled, concerns will need to be addressed, and institutional adjustments and adaptations will be warranted to ensure the feasibility of such projects, all taking into account the uniqueness of the region. Investments in most of the large potential hydropower projects in Nepal such as Karnali, Mahakali, Sapta Koshi, and West Seti and in Bhutan such as Tala and Punatsangchu would be viable only when surplus power can be exported to the vast power market of India and Bangladesh.[30] Bangladesh's rich natural gas reserve[31] would, on the other hand, only then be able to provide a base for export of gas or power based on gas production to India and on to Nepal and Bhutan. The challenges are many, calling for intense and synchronized multicountry efforts and cooperation.

In the past three years, the World Bank approved financing for three regional projects in South Asia. All projects have been classified "regional," yet they have different characteristics, scope, implementation modality, and instrumentalities. The following paragraphs discuss two select projects along with their salient features and legal, institutional, and policy difficulties encountered during preparation. These will be discussed in some detail because of the special/unique nature of the issues they raised and the manner they were addressed.

Nepal-India Electricity Transmission and Trade Project

The first example is that of the Nepal-India Electricity Transmission and Trade Project (NIETTP),[32] supported by a credit and a grant from IDA, which aimed at responding to the demand for cross-border transmission links to address power deficits in Bangladesh, India, and Nepal, and which was developed as a part of the "South Asian North East Regional Electricity Transmission and Trade Program," using the resources from IDA's regional funding mechanism. This unique purpose made it a "regional project."[33] The project was designed as one of the two projects which together secured participation by three countries (an ADB-financed Bangladesh-India project and the IDA-financed Nepal-India project), and was also designed consistently with the planned regional electricity grid of the South Asian Association for Regional Cooperation (SAARC).[34] At the time of approval of the NIETTP, the ADB-financed Bangladesh-India Project was already under implementation. This NIETTP aimed at focusing on the India and Nepal segment only. It attempted to strengthen interconnection between these two countries through a public-private partnership approach, aimed at establishing the first high-voltage (400 kilovolts) cross-border transmission interconnection between India and Nepal, capable of carrying up to 1,000 megawatts of electricity, thus facilitating electricity trade between the two countries. Upon completion, the project is expected to relieve the severe power shortages in Nepal by having India supply 150 megawatts of electricity to Nepal, and, over a longer term, stimulate investment in Nepal's hydropower sector, enabling export of surplus electricity to India.

The project includes three main components (figure 5.2), but the financing from the World Bank covers only Components B and C.

General Legal Framework

The North-South and South-North segments are expected to be built, financed, owned, and operated largely by private sector, joint-venture special-purpose companies. The Cross-border Power Transmission Company (CPTC), which is a joint venture between Power Grid Corporation of India Limited (PGCIL), the *Sutlej Jal Vidyut Nigam* Ltd (SJVNL), an Indian private sector company, and the Infrastructure Leasing and Finance Services Ltd (IL&FS), an Indian public-private infrastructure development and financing company (with the Nepal

Figure 5.2 Project Components of the Nepal-India Electricity Transmission and Trade Project

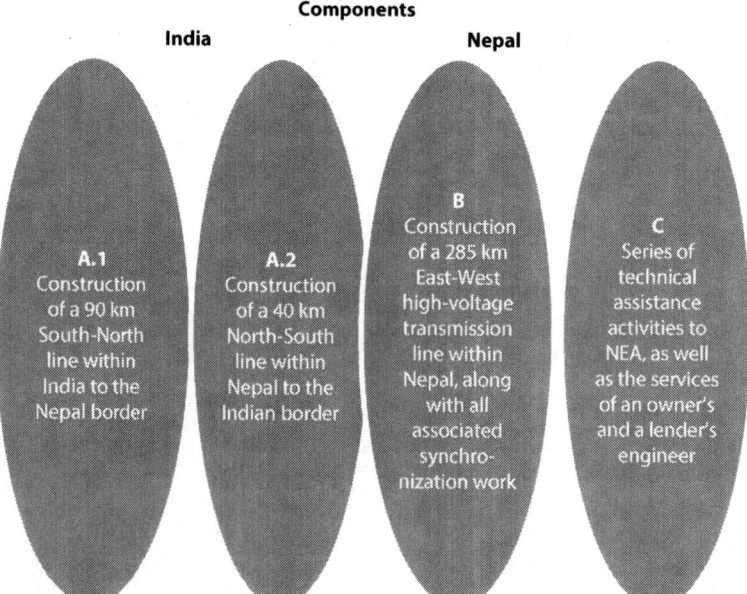

Electricity Authority (NEA) expected to take an already-authorized stake of 10 percent in CPTC), will be implementing Component A.1 of the project; and the Power Transmission Company of Nepal (PTCN), a joint venture between NEA and IL&FS, with PGCIL expected to take an already-authorized stake of 26 percent, will be implementing Component A.2 of the project.

While the corporate governance and relations among the companies will be governed by the shareholders' agreements among them and NEA's constituent instruments (in accordance with the applicable Indian and Nepalese laws as relevant), two Implementation and Transmission Services agreements (ITSAs) between NEA and CPTC, and NEA and PTCN will govern modalities of construction, operation, and cost recovery for the two North-South and South-North transmission segments. Finally, a Power Sales agreement between PTC India (formerly Power Trading Corporation, India) and NEA will govern the supply of 150 megawatts of electricity to Nepal. The signing of these three agreements was made a condition for disbursement of funds under the investment components of the NIETTP.[35]

Legal and Implementation Arrangements for the Project

As already noted above, IDA funds will only be used for Component B (East-West Transmission line, entirely within Nepal) and Component C (Technical Assistance). These components will be implemented by the NEA which, for that purpose, will receive from the Government of Nepal 50 percent of IDA financing as equity and 50 percent as a subsidiary credit (under a subsidiary agreement between the government and the NEA). These details have been reflected in the legal agreements for the NIETTP, consisting of a financing agreement between Nepal and IDA and a project agreement between IDA and NEA.

Environmental and Social Safeguards

Environmental and social safeguards have been a serious concern in Bank projects. In most private sector-sponsored large regional energy projects,[36] association with the World Bank Group is sought not necessarily only as a major source of funds but also as a major provider of comfort against country risk and as a credible certification of adherence to environmental and social norms. From this point of view, the World Bank Group practice regarding safeguard aspects appears to be a major strength. At the same time, many development practitioners also believe that conservative and rigid interpretation and application of safeguard rules and procedures are resulting in excessive requirements, deterring some private sponsors (including those pursuing energy export projects) from seeking World Bank Group participation. Many regard such application of the guidelines relating to procurement, safeguards, transparency, and resource-curse-related issues as cumulatively increasing substantially the transaction cost of doing business (box 5.6).[37]

In the NIETTP, the developers of the Nepalese and Indian sections of the transmission lines have taken separate approaches and made separate arrangements to address safeguards issues. This separation in approach was mainly

Box 5.6 Preempting Environmental and Social Safeguards

Dealing with environmental and social issues is important. Such issues can be significant, even in projects sponsored by the private sector. For example, significant issues were encountered in respect of seven IFC projects, all of which were sponsored by the private sector. Many of them attracted the attention of local, national, regional, and global nongovernmental and civil society organizations. In five of them, Bolivia-Brazil Gas Pipeline (BBGP), Baku-Tbilisi-Ceyhan Pipeline (BTC), Baku-Tbilisi-Erzurum (BTE), Nam Theun 2, and Southern Africa Gas Pipeline (SAGP), these issues were handled satisfactorily. In respect of the BTC project the Compliance Advisor/Ombudsman (CAO) of IFC received about 30 complaints from the affected parties and all of them were suitably resolved. In the case of West Africa Gas Pipeline Project (WAGP), resettlement and compensation issues led to the involvement of the Bank's inspection panel and resulted in corrective action and closer monitoring. Still disputes between the communities of the Nigerian delta region and the Nigerian Central Government remain a threat to the operation of this pipeline. Theun Hinboun Project funded by the Asian Development Bank in the early years was found to have had some adverse environmental and social impacts remaining without adequate mitigation and was attended to as a part of the expansion of the project. Complying with safeguards can be the most time-consuming and expensive part of project supervision. The clearest evidence of this is well documented in the case of the Nam Theun 2 Project and the WAGP. Most energy projects have serious safeguard issues, and hydropower projects faced more complex and often even more difficult issues. On the whole the problems seem to increase quantitatively in regional or cross-border projects, because they encompass two or more countries each with its own environmental and safeguard issues and its own systems and procedures and legal framework to deal with them. Dealing with these issues, therefore, has proven to be both challenging and expensive, yet something that cannot be undermined.

Source: Adapted from the Regional Energy Projects: Experience and Approaches of the World Bank Group, Background Paper for the World Bank Group Energy Strategy (February 2010).

justified due to different financing, regulatory, and institutional structures in the two countries. For the Nepalese sections of the transmission line, an independent environmental and social impact assessment, fully consistent with the Bank's safeguards policies, was completed and will be observed. The Indian portion, on the other hand, is expected to follow a framework approach since the exact alignment of the transmission line and locations of the towers are only being finalized at a later stage during implementation.

In order to ensure that Component A.1 (within India) is also implemented in accordance with safeguards measures acceptable to IDA, the environmental and social safeguard system of PGCIL, which was approved by IDA's board of executive directors for use for an earlier project in India (in 2009), will be used.

With respect to Component A.2 (within Nepal, but not IDA financed), an Initial Environmental Examination, a Social Management Framework, and a Vulnerable Group Development Framework have been prepared by NEA. These frameworks, which IDA has found satisfactory, include details about preparing environmental management plans, social management plans, the vulnerable group development plans, and resettlement action plans during the implementation for the project. NEA is obligated to ensure compliance with these safeguards requirements in connection with this component.

Linked Activities and Safeguards Compliance

An interesting aspect of the NIETTP is the link between its Components A.1, A.2, and B. Given that the transmission line to be constructed in both Nepal and India are directly related to the success of each other of the components, the Bank's project team initially sought to include (i) provisions binding the private parties to carry out Component A.1 in accordance with safeguard standards acceptable to IDA; and (ii) provisions allowing IDA to supervise the project, and if need be, to invoke its available remedies if the implementation of Component A.1 was not satisfactory.

In this context, therefore, a formal undertaking was sought on the part of the Indian government or the Indian state, in which the transmission line will be built to the effect that the government would (i) support the project and facilitate the task of the private companies; and (ii) allow Bank staff to visit the project site for supervision.

However, because India was not borrowing any funds from the Bank or IDA for purposes of this project, it declined to provide such an undertaking. It is noteworthy that India had taken a similar position on an ADB-financed transmission link project between Bangladesh and India. While this did represent a risk to IDA's ability to identify and remedy implementation issues (particularly safeguards-related issues) on the India side, the Bank's management opted to consider this risk modest.[38]

Regional Cooperation for Wildlife Protection

The second example concerns a regional program focusing on wildlife protection, which involved a series of country-specific projects. Designed as a horizontal APL, the projects in the series were approved and implemented in several phases. During the first phase, Bangladesh and Nepal received credits and grants, and during the second phase, Bhutan received a credit.[39] It is also expected that during the successive phases, other countries will also join (table 5.1). The regional project is defined in such a way that any country in the region can join at its own pace.

This regional program aims at focusing on a selected set of country-specific initiatives as well as key activities that are crucial to attaining regional strategic goals in the area of wildlife conservation and tackling of illegal wildlife trading.

The specific objective of the program is to assist the PCs in building and enhancing shared capacity, institutions, knowledge, and incentives to tackle illegal wildlife trade and other regional conservation threats to habitat in border areas. To meet this objective, each of the projects developed so far, as part of the first and the second phase (Bangladesh, Nepal, and Bhutan) includes two main

Table 5.1 Program Phases of the Regional Cooperation for Wildlife Protection APL

	Phase 1	Phase 2	Phase 3	Phase 4
P	Nepal			
R				
O	Bangladesh			
G		Bhutan		
R			India	
A				Vietnam;
M				Cambodia;
				Lao PDR; and other

Source: Adaptation by the author based on different project documents.

components: (i) strengthening wildlife conservation institutions and upgrading capacity to control illegal wildlife trade; and (ii) promoting wildlife conservation. More specifically, the project would finance (i) technical advisory and legal services to establish and strengthen the capacity of wildlife institutions and train their staff in the area of wildlife crime control; (ii) technical advisory services and equipment for the creation of a virtual regional center of excellence for wildlife conservation; and (iii) goods and services to carry out conservation, protection and management of protected areas and forest reserves, including (i) innovative research in wildlife conservation; (ii) pilot programs in conservation of endangered flagship species; (iii) piloting human-wildlife coexistence models and incentive schemes; (iv) development of ecotourism plans with regional conservation benefits; and (v) implementation of priority activities under such ecotourism plans.

It is important to note that the activities covered by the projects will be carried out consistent with existing international and national legal framework. For instance, the species addressed under the project are covered by the Convention on International Trade in Endangered Species (CITES), and are also part of the legislative framework of these countries.[40]

Classified as a Category "B" under the Bank's environmental classification system, the projects will not support the construction of any major new infrastructure.[41] However, considering the sensitive nature of protected areas, forest reserves, and national forests, a number of environmental safeguard polices have been triggered.[42] Similarly, while no land acquisition or resettlement is expected to be carried out under the projects, communities who traditionally rely on the protected areas for their livelihood may still be affected. In view of that fact and in order to ensure community consultations remain an integral part of project activities, the policies regarding involuntary resettlement and indigenous peoples have also been triggered. The PCs have prepared country-specific Environmental and Social Management Frameworks (ESMFs), which include measures for social risk mitigation and institutional arrangements for conducting specific social impact assessments, implementation, and monitoring. Thus, all activities financed under the projects in general, and the pilot activities included in the component, in particular, will require specific social impact assessments and mitigation measures, the ESMFs serving as a guide for all interventions. In addition, with regard to Nepal, since indigenous peoples are known to reside around virtually all protected areas, an Indigenous Peoples Development Plan Framework has been prepared as a part of the ESMF.

In the context of the program, IDA entered into separate credit and grant agreements with the three countries, at different stages of the program.

Organizational and Decision-Making Models

An efficient decision-making system is important for the success of any project. Also, in every project, organizational hierarchy and oversight affect decision making. Efficient decision making is even more important for regional projects as they involve multiple jurisdictions and sovereign authorities.

Experience clearly shows that among the factors affecting project organization are the number and variety of countries, the resource in question, and political, legal, and economic realities. It may be that even though a project organization does not present the "ideal" structure, it may be the only structure the countries have been able to agree upon, and the IDOs will have no choice but to cope with such structure. It may also be that the project structure may be the existing organizational structure of various stakeholders and their preferred ways of becoming involved in project implementation.

Based on practices of Bank-financed projects as well as operations financed by other IDOs, a pattern in decision making can be discerned. Project organizations usually have three basic levels: regional, national, and project. In addition to this, a decision-making body above a regional secretariat or implementing unit exists.

In some situations, the organizational model consists of relatively independent national organizations with weak linkages to the regional unit (figure 5.3).

Figure 5.3 Model 1—Independent National Organizations with Weak Linkages to Regional Units

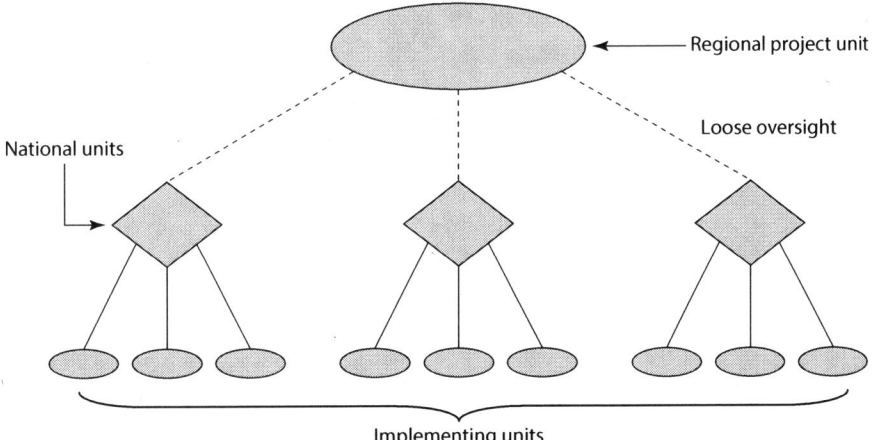

Challenges, Lessons, and Prospects for Operationalizing Regional Projects in Asia
http://dx.doi.org/10.1596/978-1-4648-0138-9

Figure 5.4 Model 2—Horizontal and Vertical Coordination among National Units

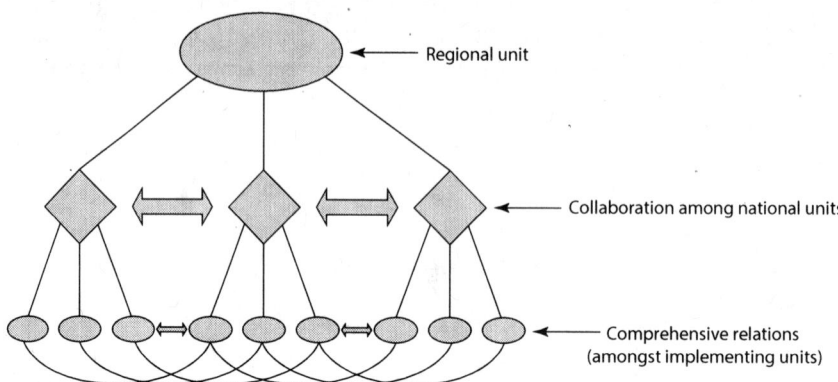

National independence allows countries to proceed at varying speeds suitable to each country. However, considering the differences between countries in the projects, in this model, making progress in addressing transboundary issues (which is often the case in a regional operation) may sometimes be delayed. This applies to both technical and policy components in project implementation. Many projects carried out in Africa appear to have followed this model (with minor and insignificant variations).

Some structures rely heavily on national coordinating units and both horizontal and vertical cooperation (figure 5.4).[43] The decision-making body consists not only of member countries but also of other relevant organizations, and in some cases governed by an international instrument. These types of organizations allow for tight contacts both horizontally and vertically. Having the implementing entities of each of the specific project components in direct contact with each other increases the effectiveness of information dissemination and quick resolution of issues concerning the program. But these structures require special attention to connections with political decision makers; otherwise, the complex network of contacts may lose its edge in catalyzing political and legislative change. They also require much from cooperating parties, including cultural, linguistic, and political closeness, as well as geographic proximity.

Also important is that in this model, a central multicountry secretariat may be helpful to operationalize actions across the project area. To ensure that the issue of legitimacy of the secretariat does not become an issue, a system to maintain it financially through the national budgets of the individual countries, will be important, along with a mandate to deal with all relevant issues. The development and negotiation of international protocols necessary to respond to cross-border issues, in addition to financially supporting the intergovernmental, interstate, and interentity structure may also be very helpful.

In this model, the regional body, through its secretariat, maintains direct contact with project units in various countries (figure 5.5).[44] The national bodies or ministries of PCs are not directly involved in project implementation and decision making. Decision making occurs through a convention (whether a formal

Figure 5.5 Model 3—Regional Secretariat Maintains Direct Contact with Project Units

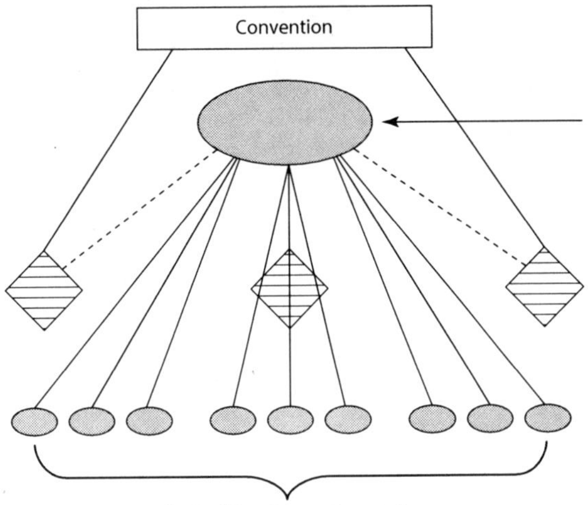

convention or an informal type) attended by all PCs, although its operationaliza-
tion needs to take place via decisions at the national level. This structure may be
especially suitable in regional projects where there is a large number of PCs. The
legally binding convention vests the project organization with authority with
respect to other PCs. Good coordination between project components and the
regional unit allows for good information flow from the project sites to the
regional office, otherwise very difficult in many regions where political problems
couch intercountry relations. This model reflects the principle of tasks having
regional dimensions being implemented at the regional level, tasks having national dimensions implemented at the national level, and tasks related to project
components implemented at the project level.

In this structure, a clear commitment for solid collaboration and cooperation
is sought at the implementation level (figure 5.6). At the top, decision making
stays separate and independent, and a formal bilateral agreement is missing. This
model is a more attractive option when political commitment at the highest level
of political decision-making level becomes impossible or inconceivable due to
difficult bilateral or multilateral relations, among PCs.[45]

In any case, before deciding on a model for an operation, it is also important
to ensure that the model chosen will pass an adequacy test. This will pertain to
the test of negotiability of the model and agreements related thereto, test of flexibility of the model, the test of sustainability, and the test of deliverability of the
model chosen. This idea and concept of test, mostly defended by negotiations
experts, is quite relevant in choosing the model.[46]

Decision making is no doubt the most critical aspect of project implementation. In regional projects, it is full of complexities on multiple technical, environmental, social, financial, legal, policy, as well as organizational fronts. The issue
of timing and multisector and multifinancier interventions bring added complexities. Moreover, many borrowing countries have weak financial or procurement

Challenges, Lessons, and Prospects for Operationalizing Regional Projects in Asia
http://dx.doi.org/10.1596/978-1-4648-0138-9

Figure 5.6 Model 4—Commitment for Collaboration at the Implementation Level

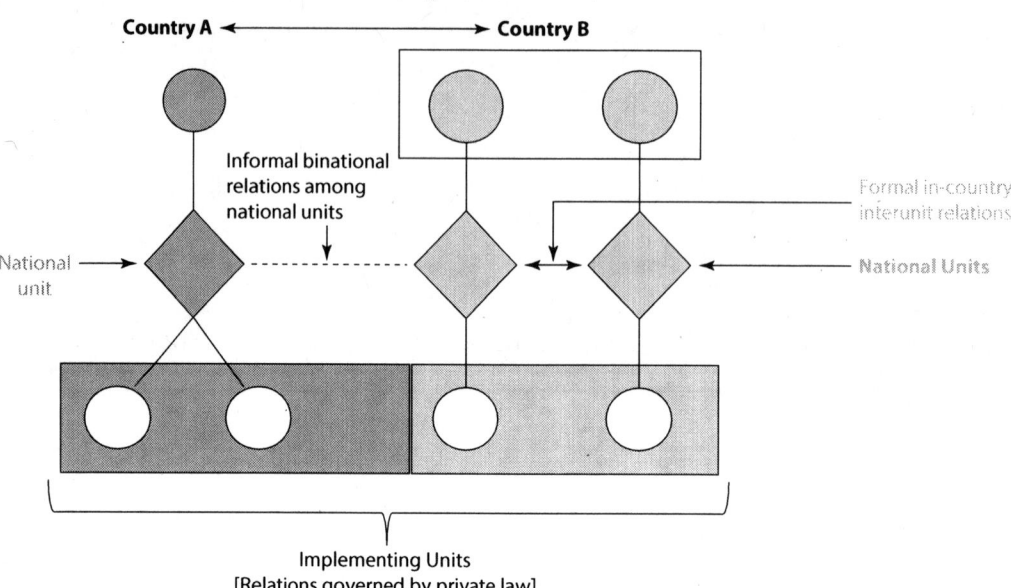

Implementing Units
[Relations governed by private law]

management capacity, which further complicates decision making. Therefore, an efficient design and delivery of complex, transformative regional operations will require the creation of a legal and institutional architecture that mitigates all the complexities, blends (without undermining) the sovereignty of the PCs, and sets up a network of unified sovereignties that enables joint and timely preparation, appraisal and implementation. These new ways of preparing, delivering complex and managing large-scale projects will demand significant new skills in government, including legal skills.[47]

Notes

1. For the purpose of this study, the term "Regional Organizations" (ROs) is used in a broad sense to cover all those organizations that incorporate international membership and encompass geopolitical or corporate entities that operationally transcend a single nation state or a single national jurisdiction. Their membership may be characterized by boundaries and demarcations characteristic to a defined and unique geography, such as continents, or geopolitics, such as economic blocks. They may have been established to foster cooperation, carry out common development activities or a joint venture, political and economic integration, or dialogue among states or entities. They may reflect both common patterns of development and history that have been fostered since decades as well as the fragmentation inherent in globalization. The definition is also meant to include all supranational entities to which countries devolve a part of their sovereign functions for purposes of delivering projects (for example, a special purpose vehicle), whether created pursuant to a treaty, agreements or even contracts, irrespective of the details and differences in the legal and constituent

instruments applicable to such creations. Also, the definition does not differentiate between donor-driven multilateral organizations and those that are aligned to and funded directly by regional member countries.

2. See also "The Development Potential of Regional Programs: An Evaluation of World Bank Support of Multicountry Operations," Submitted to the Committee On Development Effectiveness Meeting February 14, 2007 (World Bank, December 19, 2006); in particular, Appendix G: Legal Structures for Financing Regional Projects, 100–02.

3. See Georges R. Delaume, *Legal Aspects of International Lending and Economic Development Financing* (Parker School of Foreign and Comparative Law, Oceana, 1967), xviii.

4. Article V, Section 2. Articles of agreement of IDA. Moreover, whether the financing can take the form of credits or grants or both needs to be examined from the outset. Article V Section 2 (a) of IDA's Articles limits the instances in which IDA can provide financing other than loans. This Section provides that: (a) financing by the association shall take the form of loans. The Section further adds that the association may, however, provide other financing, either: (i) out of funds subscribed pursuant to Article III Section I and funds derived therefrom as principal, interest, or other charges, if the authorization for such subscription expressly provides for such financing; or (ii) in special circumstances, out of supplementary resources furnished to the association, and funds derived therefrom as principal, interest, or other charges, if the arrangements under which such resources are furnished expressly authorize such financing.

5. Article III, Section 4. Articles of agreement. Also note that in providing financing to international or regional organizations, IDA does not need to assure itself of member countries nonobjection, although it has found it prudent to do so in almost all cases. Indeed, Article V Section 2(d): In the case of a loan to an entity other than a member, *the Association may, in its discretion, require a suitable governmental or other guarantee or guarantees* (Emphasis added).

6. It is also appropriate to note that pursuant to the IDA 15 Mid Term Review of the IDA Regional Program (October 2009), discussed by the IDA Deputies, under which IDA expanded, on a pilot basis, grant financing to regional organizations. When grants are provided directly to the regional organizations, they would be subject to the same supervision, reporting, fiduciary, and evaluation rules as other IDA grants and credits extended to individual IDA member countries.

7. Reparation for Injuries Suffered in the Service of the United Nations, Advisory Opinion: I.C. J. Reports 1949, p. 174.

8. See subsequent sections in this chapter for some examples. It may be adequate to note that a detailed study on the operational aspects (including institutional processing) was carried out by the Regional Integration Department of the Africa Region. See for instance, Regional Operations Toolkit, A Resource Guide to Facilitate Design, Processing, and Implementation of Regional Projects in Africa (December 2009).

9. The nation's temperament, its sense of national destiny, its political or social ideology, or its religious sentiments have been, among other, considered as the main causes of nationalism. See, for instance, Pierre Renouvin and Jean-Baptiste Duroselle, *Introduction to the History of International Relations* (Praeger, 1964), 187–93.

10. For a detailed legal analysis, see generally, Delaume, *supra* note 3. See, for a brief discussion the World Bank Groups Financial and Legal Instruments involved in infrastructure financing, Philippe Benoit, "Infrastructure Finance—The World Bank

Group's Financial Instruments," *The Private Sector in Infrastructure. Strategy, Regulation and Risk* (World Bank, 1997), 45–49.

11. See the Project Appraisal Document 1998.

12. The Mekong River Commission (MRC) is an intergovernmental *bona fide* regional agency designated to coordinate water resources management in the Mekong River. It has four member countries: Cambodia, Lao PDR, Thailand, and Vietnam. It has the legal status and fiduciary capacity to receive grant funding and the legal authority to carry out different activities within its mandate. The agreement on Cooperation for Sustainable Development of the Mekong River Basin sets out the general objectives of cooperation which are to promote support and coordinate in the development of the full potential of sustainable benefits to all riparian states and the prevention of wasteful use of the Mekong waters. The agreement further highlights that the cooperation between the member states will be on the basis of territorial integrity in utilization and protection of the water resources of the Mekong River Basin. The agreement provides that the institutional framework for cooperation in the Mekong River Basin is the MRC and that it shall, for the purpose of the exercise of its functions, enjoy the status of an international body, including entering into agreements and obligations with the donor or international community. See the agreement establishing the MRC, Ch. IV art 11.

13. See Project Appraisal Documents in connection with the respective countries, for The Multi-country Regional Coordination on Improved Water Resources Management & Capacity Building Program.

14. In view of the fact that the project's coverage also benefitted from some coordination and collaboration of the United States' National Aeronautics and Space Administration (NASA), the Bank also notified NASA about the project, and secured, through an exchange of letters, its collaboration, in case of need.

15. Id. The Abidjan-Lagos Corridor proposal was developed by the ECOWAS Commission in partnership with the Africa Business Roundtable, with the support of the ACP Business Climate facility (BizClim) in collaboration with the African Development Bank. It is expected that the Abidjan-Lagos Corridor will stimulate free movement of goods, services, and persons and so alleviate poverty, as well as benefit the living conditions of West Africans. See *Biz News* April-June 2009/N9.

16. Ibid. See Project Appraisal Document on Proposed Credits in the Amount of SDR 85.2 Million (US$110 Million Equivalent) to Burundi, Kenya, Rwanda, Tanzania, Uganda, Zambia & African Trade Insurance Agency for a Regional Trade Facilitation Project (March 12, 2001).

17. The Nile Basin countries established, through a series of legal instruments adopted at meetings of the Nile-COM between 1999 and 2002, transitional institutional mechanisms for cooperation, including a regional organization, the NBI, headquartered in Entebbe, Uganda. The NBI institutional structure that was then established was transitional in nature until the establishment of a permanent institution within a basin-wide framework for cooperation. For a detailed analysis of the legal perspective pertaining to the cooperative framework, see Salman M. A. Salman, "The Nile Basin Cooperative Framework agreement: A Peacefully Unfolding African Spring?" *Water International* (November 2012), 1–13.

18. See The Project Appraisal Document on a Proposed Grant from the Global Environment Facility in the Amount of US$8.00 Million to the Nile Basin Initiative for Nile Transboundary Environmental Action Project (World Bank, March 5, 2003).

19. Article V Section l(d) of IDA Articles states that: "The Association shall not provide financing except upon the recommendation of a competent committee, made after a careful study of the merits of the proposal. Each such committee shall be appointed by the association and shall include a nominee of the governor or governors representing the member or members in whose territories the project under consideration is located and one or more members of the technical staff of the Association. *The requirement that the committee include the nominee of a governor or governors shall not apply in the case of financing provided to a public international or regional organization*" (Emphasis added).

    In similar vein, the IBRD Articles of agreement also provides that a Bank financing is possible only after a competent committee has submitted a written report recommending the project after a careful study of the merits of the proposal (Section 4 (iii), Article III).

20. See also Biswa Nath Bhattacharyay, "Estimating Demand for Infrastructure in Energy, Transport, Telecommunications, Water and Sanitation in Asia and the Pacific: 2010–2020," ADBI Working Paper Series No. 248 (September 2010), 21.

    Water remains one of the most important commodities for South Asia. In South Asia in particular, it is also a source of tension. Suresh Prabhu, a scholar of repute from India, considers that although a source of tensions among South Asian countries, the problems of water are not insurmountable. In fact, by recognizing the economic and hydrological interdependence of the countries of the region, mutual benefits could accrue to all countries. Neighbors have the potential to cooperate on key issues such as flood control, irrigation, power generation, and nature conservation. Prabhu appropriately notes that one of the foremost examples of regional cooperation on water is the 1960 Indus Water Treaty between India and Pakistan. In addition to the allocation of river waters to India and Pakistan, the treaty's provisions further allow for run-of-the-river hydroelectricity projects, so long as the water flows are not impounded. China's perspective is different. For China, India, and Bangladesh are both downstream and lower riparian countries. Since the Ganges and Brahmaputra river systems originate from China, water availability from these two major rivers depends on the upstream infrastructure China may build. The lack of any actual water treaty between India and China could then become a problem. On a different front, Bangladesh and India have to overcome tensions between their shared borders. They need to not only maintain but also improve their existing bilateral agreements on the Farakka Barrage and Teesta River. Bangladesh, being a lower riparian and downstream country feels aggrieved by India's water policy. In addition to grievances about water-flow levels and the lack of data sharing between India and Bangladesh, Bangladesh has also been overwhelmed by floods, water contamination, and dangerous levels of arsenic water for public consumption. Bhutan and India have a mutually beneficial agreement, where Bhutan sells electricity to India from investments made by India into Bhutan's power-generating infrastructure. The resulting royalty paid by India for this electricity accounts for almost half of Bhutan's GDP, making it one of the richest countries in the region. See, for some discussions and perspectives, Suresh P. Prabhu, "India's Water Challenges," Atlantic Council Issue Brief (October 2012). The above discussions argue strongly for a regional approach in this region on the issue of transboundary waters.

21. In this context, some scholars have noted that internationalization of infrastructure contributes to the efficiency goals of policy reform while sidestepping some political obstacles. When implemented in each nation independently, infrastructure reform can get bogged down in a quest for national advantage that undermines development for all nations in a region. In the quest for national advantage, each state is prone to favor

fledgling domestic operators rather than established foreign entities that are capable of creating an integrated regional infrastructure system. National fragmentation of infrastructure firms, especially among smaller states, further reduces the effectiveness of reform. When markets naturally cross national boundaries, a regional regulatory agreement among neighboring countries for mutual recognition of infrastructure operators facilitates the development of a seamless and competitive network. The scholars also note that electricity, telecommunications, and transportation operate more efficiently if their networks are organized according to the patterns of transactions, and trade liberalization has made these patterns increasingly international. Moreover, adjacent networks can frequently minimize costs by sharing capacity to take advantage of differences in the time pattern of usage of infrastructure services. See, for instance, Ioannis N. Kessides, Roger G. Noll, and Nancy C. Benjamin, "Regionalizing Infrastructure Reform in Developing Countries" (World Bank, Publication date unknown), 2.

22. Three countries in South Asia are landlocked: Nepal, Bhutan, and Afghanistan. In East Asia, there are two: Mongolia and Lao PDR.

23. See, "Regional Energy Projects: Experience and Approaches of the World Bank Group," Background Paper for the World Bank Group Energy Strategy (February 2010), 7. See also generally World Bank, "Asia Sustainable Energy Program," Annual Status Report (2012), and in particular page 20, which emphasizes on cross-sector regional collaboration.

24. Ibid.

25. See Anup Kumar Upadhyay, "South Asia Regional Energy Cooperation: Opportunities and Challenges," Economic Integration in South Asia (Nepal Rastra Bank, 2005), 30. The scholar, in 2005, also further noted: [D]iscounting "non-commercial" sources of energy including animal waste, wood, and other biomass, South Asia's commercial energy mix in 2002 was 46 percent coal, 34 percent petroleum, 12 percent natural gas, 6 percent hydroelectricity, 1 percent nuclear, and 0.3 percent "other." Bangladesh's energy mix, for example, is dominated by natural gas (66.4 percent in 2002), while India relies heavily on coal (54.5 percent in 2002). Sri Lanka and the Maldives are overwhelmingly dependent on petroleum (82 percent and 100 percent, respectively); Pakistan's mix is diversified among petroleum (42.7 percent), natural gas (42.2 percent), and hydroelectricity (10 percent). Bhutan and Nepal have the highest shares of hydroelectric power in their energy consumption mix at 80 percent and 31 percent, respectively. South Asian nations are faced with rapidly rising energy demand (about 10 percent per annum) coupled with increasingly insufficient energy supplies. Most of South Asia is already grappling with energy shortfalls, typically in the form of recurrent, costly, and widespread electricity outages. Because of the economic ramifications arising from such shortfalls, improving the supply of energy, particularly the supply of electricity, is an important priority of the respective governments that are looking to diversify their traditional energy supplies, promote additional foreign investment for energy infrastructure development, improve energy efficiency, reform and privatize energy sectors, and promote and expand regional energy trade and investment. See for detail, Upadhyay, South Asia Regional Energy Cooperation: Opportunities & Challenges, 36. The situation described by the scholar above has not much improved.

26. Afghanistan, Bangladesh, Bhutan, India, Maldives, Nepal, Pakistan, and Sri Lanka.

27. Bishwambher Pyakuryal and Kishor Uprety, "Economic & Legal Impact of Conflict on States & People in South Asia with Specific Reference to Nepal," *Journal of Social, Political and Economic Studies* 30, no. 4 (2005).

28. Despite the pervasive poverty of the region, South Asian nations have sophisticated industry and science sectors; thousands of years of artistic, religious and cultural development; and a large middle class. Its societies have a rich cultural tradition of unity in diversity, creative growth through human solidarity, and harmony with nature. See also, World Bank, World Development Report 2011; on the importance of regional cooperation, see also generally, Maria Perisic, "South Asia Regional Cooperation. Evolving World Bank Initiatives and the Way Forward. Trade and Transport Opportunities and Challenges," Paper presented at the Asia-Pacific Trade Facilitation Forum 2011, Seoul, Korea (October 3–8, 2011).

29. See generally, Sadiq Ahmed, Saman Kalegama, and Ejaz Ghani, eds., *Promoting Economic Cooperation in South Asia, Beyond SAFTA* (World Bank/Sage Publications, 2010). See also Prabir De, "Why is trade at borders a costly affair in South Asia? An empirical investigation," *Contemporary South Asia* 19, no.4 (December 2011): 441–64; (Routledge).

30. Shanker Krishna Malla, "Towards a Regional Energy Market in South Asia," SACEPS Paper No. 16 (May 2008), 4–5. See also, "Crisis in the Indian Power Sector," South Asia Energy Brief (December 2012), pointing to the crisis faced by the India power sector.

31. Studies by the US Geological survey have indicated the undiscovered reserves of 935 billion cubic meters (32.1 trillion cubic feet) with the reserve to production ratio of over 104 years. See Malla, *supra* note 30.

32. For detail, see generally Project Appraisal Document on a Proposed Credit in the amount of SDR 53.8 million and a proposed grant in the amount of SDR 9.7 million (US$15 million equivalent) to Nepal for a Nepal-India Electricity Transmission and Trade Project Report No: 59893-NP (World Bank, May 27, 2011).

33. It may be recalled that to be eligible to access IDA's regional funds, a project needs to be set within a regional program. See chapter 3, this volume.

34. For a brief discussion on SAARC, see chapter 6, this volume, and, in particular, Said N. Al Habsy and Kishor Uprety, "Sustaining Development and Peace South Asian Association for Regional Cooperation," International, Institutional and Legal Perspectives (University Press Limited, 2010), discussed in chapter 6, note 3, and the accompanying text.

35. In addition to the above legal instruments, a number of other legal instruments were also deemed relevant for the smooth operation of the NIETTP, particularly in enabling all the concerned companies to carry out their responsibilities. They included, among other: (i) a Joint Development agreement between NEA and IL&FS; (ii) Certificates of incorporation of the joint-venture companies; (iii) the License from the Ministry of Industry authorizing foreign investment in the project and the joint venture agreements; (iv) a Memorandum of agreement between NEA and PTCP, PTCN, CPTC for the sale of surplus power to PTC, and make up for the shortfall by buying power through PTC on commercial basis; and (vi) an Arrangement for the sale of power between NEA and PTC on a long-term basis.

    For a deeper understanding of the different legal instruments involved in projects, in various sectors, and where private sector financing is also involved, see generally, Benoit, *The Private Sector in Infrastructure, supra* note 10.

36. Such as Bolivia-Brazil Gas Pipeline (BBGP), Baku-Tbilisi-Ceyhan Pipeline (BTC), Baku-Tbilisi-Erzurum (BTE), and Southern Africa Gas Pipeline (SAGP).

37. See for detailed discussions, "Regional Energy Projects: Experience and Approaches of the World Bank Group," Background Paper for the World Bank Group Energy Strategy (February 2010).

38. Mainly because of the following three considerations:
    1. The significant influence PGCIL exercises over CPTC which has been set up to build and operate the transmission line on the India side; an influence attributable to the fact that PGCIL represents the interest of India's public sector enterprises which own 52 percent of CPTC, and PGCIL's interest in protecting its own reputation
    2. The CPTC shareholders' agreement which requires the observance of safeguards policies that are in line with those of PGCIL's Environmental and Social Policies and Procedures (ESSP) (used in an earlier project), and the fact PGCIL applies ESSP for all its investments, regardless of the financing source; and
    3. The size of the investment in India which is small, and the line routing which would traverse an area without significant safeguard risks and with sufficient scope for mitigating social and environmental impacts. Furthermore, the line length of the project about 90 kilometers is small compared to 325 kilometers (plus substations) on the Nepal side, and compared to more than 5,000 kilometers of high-voltage transmission lines installed annually in India by PGCIL.

39. See Project Appraisal Document on a Proposed Credit in the Amount of SDR 22.9 Million to the People's Republic of Bangladesh & A Proposed Grant in the Amount of SDR 2.0 Million to Nepal in Support of the First Phase of the APL on Strengthening Regional Cooperation for Wildlife Protection in Asia, World Bank Report No: 59962-SAS (March 11, 2011). Also, within a period of two to three years, a number of other South and East Asian countries are also expected to participate (India, Lao PDR, and Vietnam). For detail, see Project Appraisal Document on a Proposed Credit in the Amount of SDR 1.4 Million to the Kingdom of Bhutan in Support of the Second Phase of the APL on Strengthening Regional Cooperation for Wildlife Protection in Asia, World Bank Report No: 62116-SAS (May 26, 2011).

40. CITES, the Convention on International Trade in Endangered Species of Wild Fauna and Flora, is an international agreement between governments. Its aim is to ensure that international trade in specimens of wild animals and plants does not threaten their survival. CITES was drafted pursuant to a resolution adopted in 1963 at a meeting of members of IUCN (International Union for the Conservation of Nature). The text of the convention was agreed at a meeting of representatives of 80 countries in Washington DC., United States of America, on 3 March 1973, and on 1 July 1975 CITES entered in force. Countries adhere voluntarily to CITES and such countries are known as Parties. Although CITES is legally binding on the Parties, it does not take the place of national laws. Rather, it provides a framework to be respected by each Party, which has to adopt its own domestic legislation to ensure that CITES is implemented at the national level. See Text of the Convention.

41. Under its Policy (Operational Policy 4.01), the World Bank classifies a proposed project into one of four categories, depending on the type, location, sensitivity, and scale of the project and the nature and magnitude of its potential environmental impacts.
    1. A proposed project is classified as Category A if it is likely to have significant adverse environmental impacts that are sensitive, diverse, or unprecedented. These impacts may affect an area broader than the sites or facilities subject to physical works. Environmental assessment for a Category A project will examine the project's potential negative and positive environmental impacts, compare them with

those of feasible alternatives (including the "without project" situation), and recommend any measures needed to prevent, minimize, mitigate, or compensate for
adverse impacts and improve environmental performance.

2. A proposed project is classified as Category B if its potential adverse environmental impacts on human populations or environmentally important areas—including
wetlands, forests, grasslands, and other natural habitats—are less adverse than
those of Category A projects. These impacts are site-specific; few if any of them
are irreversible; and in most cases mitigation measures can be designed more readily than for Category A projects.

3. A proposed project is classified as Category C if it is likely to have minimal or no
adverse environmental impacts. Beyond screening, no further environmental
assessment action is required for a Category C project.

4. A proposed project is classified as Category FI if it involves investment of World
Bank funds through a financial intermediary, in subprojects (second tier investments for activities that are yet unknown but will be developed in the course of
implementation) that may result in adverse environmental impacts.

42. Environmental Assessment; Natural Habitats; and Forests.

43. The WARFP is an example of a project following this model. For other examples following this model, in particular, projects dealing with regional global environmental
challenges, see also, *Making Development Sustainable* (in particular Chapter 4, Part 1),
World Bank (1994), 126–30.

44. The Senegal River Basin MWRD Project would, for instance, fall into this category.
Also the Wildlife Protection Project has been quite close to following this model. For
other examples following this model, see also, *Making Development Sustainable, supra*
note 43.

45. This has been the model followed in the regional projects in South Asia, namely the
NIETTP discussed earlier in this chapter.

46. The idea, due to its relevance, is borrowed and adapted from literature on negotiations. See, for example, Russel B. Sunshine, *Negotiating for International Development*
(Martinus Nijhof, 1990), 110–14.

47. See, generally, "Modernizing the Delivery of Complex Transformational Regional
(Infrastructure) Project in Africa," First Discussion Draft, Regional Integration
Department (March 1, 2013), 16–17.

CHAPTER 6

Uniqueness and Challenges for Asia

In addition to the decision-making models discussed in chapter 5, and notwithstanding the different considerations ensuing from the examples touched upon by the earlier chapters, a common pattern and an approach in designing regional projects can be discerned in a broad manner. But for Asia, and in particular for South Asia, the approach may call for further adaptations. The following paragraphs will attempt to show some of the specific issues and challenges pertaining to Asia.

Incongruity of Technical Engagement and Political Commitment

All countries in the region, separately, and even collectively in selected international fora, agree on the need for cooperating and collectively developing projects that will be beneficial for all. Technically, that is possible, but politically, the situation is quite different. Issues of sovereignty, sharing of benefits, perceptions of hegemony, long- and short-term adverse impacts, and so forth continue to dominate decision making. Decision makers still continue to each think of their country as a separate entity, rather than as a part of a region, which, as a whole, is a unit.

As such, a clearly articulated commitment, an enabling policy environment, and a mechanism to help translate policies and public statements into actions and then monitor their implementation built on lessons learnt are still missing. Such commitments do not seem irreconcilable since, notwithstanding the various differences in the political development of the South Asian countries, certain common "trends" and "waves" can be easily noticed. The problems and needs of these countries, as well as their goal of development, are, by and large, the same.

Weak Regional Framework and Enabling Environment

At the outset, it seems interesting to note that, according to a recent report, in contrast with the Asia region, regional approaches have been game changers for many African countries.[1] And this, in the author's view, is also due to the multiple layers of existing enabling legal framework in Africa facilitating the undertaking, by multiple countries, of regional projects, although the capacity and the authority to oversee is still relatively weak and the continent still largely operates sub-regionally and with insufficient enforcement mechanism.[2]

Unlike in Africa and Europe, for instance, an all-encompassing multilateral treaty, facilitating development of the region as a whole and a clear legal framework providing an enabling environment for developing regional projects does not, in reality, exist in Asia. More specifically, relations among the South Asian countries are essentially governed by bilateral treaties, in parallel with the South Asian Association for Regional Cooperation (SAARC), a regional institution,[3] and among the East Asian countries, in addition to different bilateral agreements, in parallel with the Association of Southeast Asian Nations (ASEAN), another international organization. And both organizations, from the perspective of regional projects, suffer from their own types of limitations, although ASEAN seems to be relatively more efficient. The following few brief introductory paragraphs introduce these two organization to understand the context.

SAARC and Its Difficulties

SAARC was established in 1985 by seven South Asian nations to facilitate regional cooperation in a wide range of areas and to cooperate with international organizations pursuing similar goals. Its eighth South Asian member joined later (Afghanistan). This organization considers regional cooperation a complement to bilateral relations of member states, but does not explicitly recommend and promote real regional endeavors. Moreover, bilateral or contentious issues are excluded from SAARC deliberations. This exclusion further complicates the matter and, as a result, the institution lacks clout among its member states, preventing it from realizing its full potential. The SAARC Secretariat (located in Kathmandu) is very small, with about 30 staff members. Member states are responsible for implementing SAARC's different initiatives, many of which do not progress due to lack of resources and political backing. Certainly, SAARC has facilitated the implementation of some regional economic and social cooperation agenda, but has not been able to influence regional geopolitics, and thus drive the development agenda.

One should not, however, underestimate SAARC's huge convening power. Indeed, after its establishment, various actions and measures have been taken by the South Asian countries in the context of fostering cooperation and regional development. It has played an important role in shaping and formulating a number of international law instruments (conventions, protocols, and agreements) through and within its framework. For the formalization of cooperation among countries in the region, under its auspices, countries have developed different legal instruments, essentially aimed at improving economic and social areas, regulating security interests, providing food security, enhancing trade, combating social evils such as flesh trade, promoting child welfare, and defending specific security concerns of these countries in a more effective and concerted manner. But for all practical purposes, and in view of its constituent instruments (the charter), SAARC cannot be an implementer: it can only be a facilitator, with the added benefit that it remains a low-cost, low-risk platform for promoting regional cooperation on sociocultural and economic and technical issues. In this context, SAARC has established two regional centers in Bangladesh (agriculture and meteorological), two in India (documentation and disaster management), two in Nepal (tuberculosis and information), two in Pakistan (human resources development and energy), one in Sri Lanka (cultural), one in Maldives (coastal zone management), and one in Bhutan (forestry). Its eleven regional centers are separately developing concrete plans to advance its regional action plans, but implementation depends on member states, many of which lack capacity and, as noted above, resources.

One additional noteworthy creation, with relevance to financing of development, within this organization is the SAARC Development Fund (SDF). Created with the objective of promoting the welfare of the people of the region, improving the quality of life, and accelerating economic growth, social progress, and poverty alleviation in the region, it has a secretariat based in Bhutan.[4]

ASEAN's Proactivity

ASEAN, another organization which shares goals relatively similar to SAARC, is in a relatively advanced stage from an institutional perspective. ASEAN was made operational in 1967 (more than 20 years before the formation of SAARC) by its five original member countries, namely, Indonesia, Malaysia, the Philippines, Singapore, and Thailand, through the "ASEAN Declaration" signed by five foreign ministers in Bangkok on August 8, 1967.[5] Brunei Darussalam joined in 1984, Vietnam in 1995, Lao People's Democratic Republic (Lao PDR) and Myanmar in 1997, and Cambodia in April 1999. The ASEAN Declaration states that the aims and purposes of the association are to accelerate economic growth, social progress, and cultural development in the region and to promote regional peace and stability through abiding respect for justice and the rule of law in the relationship among countries in the region and adherence to the principles of the United Nations Charter. It was around that time that the leaders of Thailand, Indonesia, the Philippines, and Malaysia realized that the time had come for them to close ranks or risk a future mired in turmoil and confrontation. The alternative was for the region to remain fragmented and for each country to remain vulnerable to external powers. They recognized that their fragmented economies had little chance of expansion individually from the onslaught of powerful economies around them unless they pooled their untapped potentials and defended themselves against negative influences from outside the region.

It was only during the 13th ASEAN Summit in Singapore, in November 2007, while celebrating the 40th anniversary of the organization's founding, that the leaders of ASEAN nations formally signed a charter, thus transforming the organization into a rule-based entity.

The 2007 charter formally provides the basis for ASEAN's legal and institutional framework for contribution toward peace, progress, and prosperity of the region. Forty years after ASEAN's inception, when the countries of the region

Challenges, Lessons, and Prospects for Operationalizing Regional Projects in Asia
http://dx.doi.org/10.1596/978-1-4648-0138-9

have made significant economic and political advancements, the 10 heads of states and governments got together to sign the charter to give the organization a legal personality and codify the key principles and goals of ASEAN.[6] With the motto "one vision, one identity, one community," the ASEAN member states have consciously agreed to submit themselves to the principles of the association.

The charter, enumerating the purpose of the organization, declares that member states will maintain peace and stability, resolve all disputes amicably, enhance regional resilience, keep the region free of nuclear weapons, and strengthen peace-oriented values in the region. It goes on to state that member states shall create a single market in which there is free flow of goods, services, and investments and facilitated movement of people and labor. It also emphasizes the need to alleviate poverty and strengthen democracy, human rights, and fundamental freedoms. In short, it touches all aspects of human development making the organization more people oriented. However, the desire to create an "ASEAN Economic Community" is, perhaps, the most significant step the leaders have decided upon.

The most interesting provision of the charter is in Article 20, which states that decision making in ASEAN will be based on consultation and consensus. There is no requirement of unanimity for making decisions, as is the case with the SAARC Charter. This procedure, indeed, releases the organization from being hamstrung. The principle of "consensus" gives it the necessary flexibility to make decisions that are needed to move the organization forward.

From an institutional angle, the highest decision-making organ of ASEAN is the Meeting of the ASEAN Heads of State and Government. The ASEAN Summit is convened every year. The ASEAN Ministerial Meeting (Foreign Ministers) is held annually. Ministerial meetings on the following sectors are also held regularly: agriculture and forestry, economics (trade), energy, environment, finance, health, information, investment, labor, law, regional haze, rural development and poverty alleviation, science and technology, social welfare, telecommunications, transnational crime, transportation, tourism, and youth. Supporting these ministerial bodies are committees of senior officials, technical working groups, and task forces.

ASEAN has several specialized bodies and arrangements promoting intergovernmental cooperation in various fields including an Agricultural Development Planning Centre, an ASEAN-EC Management Centre, a Centre for Energy, an Earthquake Information Centre, a Foundation, a Poultry Research and Training Centre, a Regional Centre for Biodiversity Conservation, a Rural Youth Development Centre, a Specialized Meteorological Centre, a Timber Technology Centre, a Tourism Information Centre, and a University Network.

SAARC Versus ASEAN

There is no doubt that ASEAN has been more effective than SAARC in the production of regional security and order.[7] Since its formation, ASEAN members have not used military force to resolve interstate disputes. This does not, however, mean that the region is devoid of conflicts. There are unresolved security prob-lems, both territorial- and identity based, but they have not provoked hostilities, and despite its weak formal mandate for resolving conflicts, ASEAN's presence has made for a more orderly Southeast Asia. ASEAN has developed over the years into a working diplomatic community, and while it has concurrently grown in international stature, consultation and cooperation within ASEAN have cre-ated a zone of peace of a limited but valuable kind in comparison with the cir-cumstances of the early 1960s. Actually, some scholars have noted that ASEAN facilitated the transformation of a subregion of turmoil into a more stable area in which the role of force has been minimized, though not eliminated.[8] In the SAARC region, in contrast, the use of military force has still remained an option, as was evident in 1999 when Pakistan and India fought the Kargil War. Both countries also amassed troops on their borders in 2002. Also, common member-ship of SAARC has not modified perceptions and behavior of some of its mem-bers, whose relations are bedeviled by deep mistrust and antagonism.[9]

A detailed comparison between SAARC and ASEAN is beyond the scope of this study. Nonetheless, a limited attempt to understand the two in the context of general development may not be unwarranted. Actually, their effectiveness, particularly in the context of conflict management, has been subjected to consid-eration by many analysts, who have been able to isolate elements serving as comparators, and entailing success or failure of each one. Such elements are also relevant indicators when comparing their effectiveness in general. These include, among others, (i) formal and informal modalities of interaction; (ii) consensus in ASEAN decision-making process; (iii) shared perceptions and values; (iv) asym-metry of countries and its effect on the organizational decision making; (v) extra-regional actors as contributing or constraining factors; (vi) the culture of cooperation in ASEAN creating an enabling environment; and (vii) leadership.[10]

Whatever the circumstances and reasons, the fact remains that SAARC (with a charter from the beginning), compared to ASEAN (operating without a charter for many years), has been much less effective, not only in managing conflict but also in generating development flow.[11] This suggests that "informal means" and "unwritten political commitment" can also, in certain circumstances, effectively take forward a development agenda. But in any case, depending on the specific situation of the region or countries, International Development Organizations (IDOs) approach in designing regional projects should take into account the dif-ferences so as to be able to always propose workable solutions.[12]

Lengthy Process of Treaty Making

Generally, treaty making involves a long process. Its negotiation segment is even more challenging as it involves almost every facet of the relationship among and between states. Completing a treaty can also be time- and cost consuming because of the number of details that need to be worked out. Furthermore, the sequences involved in the process—preliminary studies, preparation of the initial drafts, negotiations, consultations, adoption, and so forth—take time and do not necessarily help in accelerating the pace of development needs of countries. The overall process is even longer when it involves more than two countries. And this process fares worse when it comes to South Asia, a region where the treaty making process is, at best, poorly coordinated, and where tensions between, and among, countries loom large and delay any outcome. Competence to deal with particular questions exists simultaneously in different agencies of the different governments. The pace of success, as such, often depends on chance, on the topic, and on obscure political considerations that lead interested states to a specific approach and compromise, and eventually to the outcome. Because of these ground realities, the development partners need to be even more creative and find alternative solutions to deal with the existing challenges.

Notes

1. See World Bank, "Africa's Future and the World Bank's Support to It" (March 2011a), 30.

2. Also, note that as per an internal document of the World Bank, the Africa Regional Integration portfolio is large and complex with commitments of US$6 billion for regional infrastructure, institutional cooperation and regional public goods programs. Roughly 45 percent of this portfolio is in energy, 25 percent in transport and trade facilitation, 12 percent in ICT, 9 percent in agriculture, 7 percent in water and environment, and the rest is in finance and health. Several large and complex transformative multicountry programs and projects are likely to enter the portfolio in coming years. See also generally, "Modernizing the Delivery of Complex Transformational Regional (Infrastructure) Project in Africa," First Discussion Draft, Regional Integration Department (March 1, 2013),in particular, Annex 2.

3. For detailed discussions, see generally, Said N. Al Habsy and Kishor Uprety, *Sustaining Development and Peace: South Asian Association for Regional Cooperation, International, Institutional and Legal Perspectives* (University Press Limited, 2010).

4. For detailed discussions, see Al Habsy and Uprety, *supra* note 3.

5. For some brief discussion, see Ralph H. Folsom, Michael Wallace Gordon, and John A. Spanogle Jr., *International Business Transactions* (West Publishing, 1992), 389–404.

6. The charter, along with its 13 chapters, 55 articles, and 4 annexes, was drafted by representatives of all the 10 member states and is designed to meet the challenges of the twenty-first century, thus making ASEAN an undisputed regional player of the Asia-Pacific region.

    ASEAN comprises ten countries: Brunei Darussalam, Cambodia, Indonesia, Lao PDR, Malaysia, Myanmar, the Philippines, Singapore, Thailand, and Vietnam, and has 10 dialogue partners, including Australia, Canada, China, European Union, India, Japan, New Zealand, the Republic of Korea, the Russian Federation, and the United States. The United Nations Development Program also holds a dialogue status.

7. See generally, Mohamad Faisol Keling, Hishamudin Md.Som, Mohamad Nasir Saludin, Md. Shukri Shuib, and Mohd Na'eim Ajis, "The Development of ASEAN from Historical Approach," *Asian Social Science* 7, no. 7 (July 2011): 169–89.

8. See generally, Ibid., 182.

9. See Al Habsy and Uprety, *supra* note 3.

10. While both suffer from intraregional asymmetries, these are considerably more acute in SAARC Region than in ASEAN. Indonesia's (the largest ASEAN member in terms of size and population) GDP is 0.6 times, its territory 0.7 times, and its population 0.6 times larger than all the other ASEAN members combined. By comparison India's territory is 1.8 times, population 2.9 times, armed forces personnel 1.5 times, and military expenditure 4.5 times larger than the other SAARC member countries combined. Disparity is huge. India, for instance, towers over its South Asian neighbors in terms of territorial size and population, GDP, and military power. See for a detailed comparative study, Amitabh Acharya, "ASEAN and SAARC: Comparing Experiences and Sharing Lessons" (unpublished draft report dated June 15, 2012) presented at a World Bank Workshop, on April 15, 2013, 5.

11. As interestingly observed by a scholar, while South Asia is stuck at the "second" stage of regionalism (meaning at preliminary stage, as per some scholarly classifications), Southeast Asia has become a *regional* society already. The scholar notes that the network of regional organizations in South Asia has not impacted upon the regional environment. It has neither contributed to creating a security community, nor has it contributed to evolving developmental complementarities. For the scholar, South Asia continues to remain a peripheral region. As against this, regionalization of Southeast Asia has been far more successful, both in terms of deepening and widening, its notable success being in terms of regional security. The scholar considers it difficult to be optimistic about the future of regionalization of South Asia, which is more likely to decline, and believes South Asia as a viable region, will be dissolved. On the other hand, Southeast Asia has emerged as a more coherent region and a force to reckon with. See, Uttara Sahasrabuddhe, "Regionalisation Processes in South and Southeast Asia: A Comparative Study" (Undated paper), 8–9.

12. See some proposals in chapter 7, this volume.

Challenges, Lessons, and Prospects for Operationalizing Regional Projects in Asia
http://dx.doi.org/10.1596/978-1-4648-0138-9

Prospects and Proposals

The United Nations Secretary General, Ban Ki Moon, notes:

> [T]he currents of change are transforming our human and physical geography. Demographic transformation, the emergence of new centers of economic dynamism, accelerating inequality within and across nations, challenges to the existing social contract by a disillusioned, mobilized citizenry, technological and organizational transformation linking people directly as never before and climate change, are all placing the foundations of our world and our global system under unprecedented stress. They are driving not just incremental but exponential change. They are deeply connected and increasingly complex. To ensure that our generation and future generations benefit from the opportunities presented by this changing reality and are able to mitigate increased risks, the global community will need to work together in unprecedented ways. [1]

The statement above is quite relevant for the Bank and its recent agenda, which is in favor of, and focuses on, regional projects.[2] But the problems of regional development are legion, and this paper can only touch upon select aspects. In view of the uniqueness of each situation and based on our experience, if promoting regional projects were to be the institutional priority, it does not seem practical to take an approach that demands strict compliance vis-a-vis the requirements of a regional project. Also, it does not seem feasible to always take the same approach in all regions. Each region is unique; each country is unique. A decision based on lessons learnt, best practices, and the principles of efficiency and rapidity may, therefore, be more useful. The following paragraphs make a few proposals to help respond to the unique situation, all having to deal with legal and institutional aspects.

Compensating for Treaty-Making Delays

Indeed, in all international relations and transactions, one important concern pertains to the existence of binding international treaties. A treaty is one of the recognized sources of international law.[3] Its binding force follows from the customary maxim of *pacta sunt servanda*, which ultimately reflects state sovereignty limited through consent. The violation of duties under a treaty counts as a breach of international law, incurring state responsibility and the possibility of sanctions, often defined in the treaty itself as part of a negotiated compliance mechanism. While offering a high degree of certainty, the adoption of an international treaty entails a lengthy and often contentious ratification process. Likewise, subsequent amendments to the treaty or a withdrawal from it are again subject to sophisticated rules of international law. Nonetheless, due to the formal nature and the transparency they offer, international treaties are likely the most reliable instrument of choice for all arrangements. But as treaty making can be a very lengthy process, attempts to secure commitments in some other form, sometimes, need to be made.

The second concern is the reciprocity of commitments. Rather than approving an international arrangement with binding force, countries could also enter a political commitment to adopt reciprocal legislation within their respective jurisdictions, thereby ensuring the mutual recognition of the objectives. Such an arrangement would ultimately entail an adaptation of the respective platform systems and thus derive its authority from domestic law, although it would result from formal or informal negotiations and preparatory meetings between states. Relative to an international treaty, of course, such a construction would not have the capacity to bind participating jurisdictions beyond the country whose domestic law is invoked, and would allow for unilateral amendment or termination of the overall objective without prior consent of other parties.

A final vehicle for establishing and maintaining a link among countries for a common goal is contractual arrangements under private law, that is, the law governing the mutual relations between natural and legal persons, notably the law of contracts and torts,[4] or the law of obligations.[5] This concept is also attractive to many, although it will involve some form of contract, either to establish a longer contractual relationship or purely negotiated *in casu* to govern individual operational transactions. Whether a formal link with the highest political authority has been created or not, transactions leading to a common venture will generally involve a contract specifying the terms of a particular venture, such as the cost, the completion date, a force majeure clause, and default or liability provisions, and can become enforceable at implementation level.

Unlike public international law, private law is not a body of norms adopted across national frontiers. Instead, it differs from state to state, often with vast differences between historically separate regulatory traditions such as the common law, which is largely based on judicial precedent, and civil law, which is largely based on codified rules. In the absence of a harmonized normative framework, the contractual arrangements will thus be governed either by the private law of a particular state as specified in the contract, the most likely case, or by the private law of the state determined by way of international private law. This latter set of rules, also known as conflict of laws, merely helps regulate transboundary relations between private law subjects by determining which of the competing legal systems is applicable. The choice of law in contractual relationships is typically selected based upon either the place where the transaction physically occurred (*lex loci actus*) or the doctrine of the proper law, which is the law with the closest connection to the facts of the case.

However, this altogether allows for great flexibility in the development of an operation based on private law, although the scope of application tends to remain limited to individual transactions. As mentioned earlier, cross-border participants are likely to insist on a transparent, legally binding framework for transactions between their respective jurisdictions for their operations, favoring the predictability of formal legislation over a contractual solution based on private law, but in a situation where such a framework is not feasible, the private law route may become handy.

Using Soft Instruments

Whenever formal legal enabling instruments are not available, during preparation of regional projects, International Development Organization (IDOs) should not hesitate to endorse the use of soft legal instruments. This terminology remains somewhat controversial in international law, since some international practitioners do not accept its existence and others consider its status in the realm of law to be unclear. However, for most international practitioners, development of soft law instruments is an accepted part of the compromises required when undertaking daily work within the international legal system, where states are often reluctant to sign up formally to too many commitments that might result in national resentment at overcommitting to an international goal. From an IDO's perspective, therefore, the approach of soft framework may help address the impediments emanating from the need to secure hard laws in place before developing any regional projects.

Enhancing Risk Taking

Some difficulties that arise in developing regional projects are also related to the fact that IDOs, such as the World Bank, bound by their internal policies, are somewhat risk averse, and thus hesitate to take even risks that are not significant and unmanageable. Unlike many private sector corporations, where risk taking is part of the trade, an international organization like the World Bank naturally prefers to operate in a "safe" environment, that is only after ensuring that all legal instruments (regardless of their importance) are in place. As a result, it takes a long time for a project to come to fruition and the opportunity cost of preparation escalates for countries as well as development partners, which consequently becomes a disincentive for doing new regional projects, defending regional agenda. Therefore, adopting new policies and practices that allow for more risk taking, based on analysis of each and every case, could provide an incentive for regional projects.[6]

Challenges, Lessons, and Prospects for Operationalizing Regional Projects in Asia
http://dx.doi.org/10.1596/978-1-4648-0138-9

Relying on the Market

The IDOs often show a tendency of getting involved in all upstream and down-stream effects of projects they finance. Protection of rights and interests of all member countries is an integral part of their modus operandi. In most cases, the responsibility for ensuring a required order is placed on governmental agencies, or on independent self-regulating professional organizations. IDOs like the World Bank operate to protect their own rights, the rights of member countries and those of the borrowers, and to respect their policies. All these requirements emanating from the philosophy of good governance essentially from a public sector perspective, actually, have the effect of delaying the development of regional projects. Hence, for regional projects, especially when developed in partnership with private sector companies, it may be worthwhile to also rely on private sector practices and let the market decide on many of the risks.[7] In such scenarios, from a legal standpoint, it would be important to pay particular attention to address the issues concerning conflict of laws (broadly encompassing choice of law and constitutional or legal limitations on the choice), as well as the issues pertaining to the jurisdictions of courts, recognition of foreign judgments, and exequatur.

The most important goal for both enhancement of risk taking and reliance on market is more proactive risk management. In other words, an adequate risk allocation to the party who is best placed to manage it (whether public or private sector).[8]

Indirect Leveraging

Often, by dealing with a few local partners and creating obligations on them, development partners can achieve what they ought to achieve. Development partners can require the local parties to their agreements to comply with a number of obligations pertaining to taking actions that would otherwise need to be taken by the development partners for them to comply with their own fiduciary obligations. This technique of ensuring rights by proxy can help facilitate negotiations and development of regional projects, since the majority of the recipient parties or private investors will feel less pressured by obligations vis-a-vis an international development partner. A consequential additional advantage of this is that it will not force borrowers' governments to seek alternative sources of financing with fewer obligations.

Multifaceted Intervention

While developing a regional project, it is important to ensure that the intervention is multifaceted, multisided, and multisector. This approach may help manage the perception (suspicion) of limitedness that a specific country may have if only one sector were to become the target of intervention. In this context, it will further help to develop a common approach among donors, and for efficiency purposes, for all development partners to be involved at a very early stage of preparation as well as to synchronize their intervention.

The typology of projects may be in the form of (i) local (covering a small area, operating, for example, at local authority level); (ii) regional (within larger spatial units, usually defined by administrative boundaries or natural features); (iii) cross-border (between states, but tending to be on quite a small scale confined to the areas close to the borders); (iv) transregional and transnational (comprehensive, covering an area of cooperation formed by connected regions or nations); and (v) interregional (between a number of regions that are not directly physically connected).

However, a word of caution seems warranted. Multifaceted intervention should become an approach only when it does not result in complicating regional projects more. It has to be only if and when it helps in facilitating the undertaking.[9]

Incentivizing Regionalism

The development partners, within their own institutional apparatus and modus operandi should create incentives for staff and units catering to regional projects. Institutions that have long focused on traditional nonregional projects should develop a system in which more funds are made available for projects with a focus on regional agenda, and create incentives for staff that are involved in preparing, and supervising the management and the implementation of such regional projects, which often take longer to complete than other traditional (nonregional) projects.

Creating Constituencies for Regional Projects

There is, perhaps, also a need to create a support base of people and countries that can recognize the significance of going "regional" and pursuing their interests through regional projects, including, without limitation, community support organizations, private sector or even stakeholders. Attracting these constituencies will require a bottom-up process that encourages active participation and promotes confidence in the stability of regional programs. Such a bottom-up process should be always in consideration in designing a regional operation.[10]

Clarifying Cross-Border Roles and Responsibilities

The need for cross-border coordination has derailed many projects that are economically attractive.[11] As such, in developing a regional project, especially cross-border projects or those involving international transport corridors, it is also important to consider operations functions early on. Early consideration of functional and jurisdictional roles can help the implementation and avoid conflict at a later stage (often cross-border). Broadly, these functions can be divided in three categories: (i) national functions that are the responsibility of an individual

Challenges, Lessons, and Prospects for Operationalizing Regional Projects in Asia
http://dx.doi.org/10.1596/978-1-4648-0138-9

agency in one specific country where the project, or part thereof, will be based and which can be viewed as those that the agency would be doing anyway even if it had no involvement in cities across the border; (ii) national/regional functions that are those carried out by the national agency, without interagency collaboration but which would regionally benefit the project if done with a regional perspective; and (iii) purely regional functions that are performed for both regional and national benefits and cannot be performed without regional cooperation and collaboration between two agencies or an international agency.

Once the respective roles and responsibilities are well determined, a mechanism to ensure accountability from the entities needs to also be developed. Determining and using accountability as a monitoring indicator will help mitigate the risks in a more visible manner.

Adopting Flexibility

In parallel to the formalized systems, an informal system to allow the regional and local partners on all sides of the border to analyze their common needs and to identify priorities and actions that are most relevant to their local situation should be developed. The management of the programs could be entrusted to a local or national authority jointly selected by all Participating Countries (PCs).

It may also be worth using an approach which follows "Structural Funds" principles.[12] This would involve, for instance, multiannual programming, partnership, and cofinancing, adapted to take into account the specificities of the different countries' external relations rules and regulation. The programs involving regions and countries on all sides and borders may also share one single-budget, common management structures, a common legal framework and implementation rules giving the program a fully balanced partnership among the PCs.

Supporting and Developing Regional Organizations

Inevitably, there will be rebuttal, rhetoric, and resistance from those holding opposing views about the significant development-related role regional organizations (ROs) can assume, but the time has come to also encourage the creation of ROs or to support them energetically including by giving them a secure financial base to develop their institution capacities.[13] This will have multiple advantages. First, the ROs may become an efficient vehicle and an institutional facilitator in the implementation of the regional integration agenda countries have set for themselves. Second, in addition to being an active player in development and a vehicle for channeling of funds, regional organizations can also be useful in providing the best possible check and balance against abuses in development from all sides.

Notes

1. United Nations, "The Secretary-General's Five-Year Action Agenda" (January 25, 2012). http://www.un.org/sg/priorties/sg-agenda-2012.pdf.

2. See also discussions chapter 3, this volume.

3. Art. 38, Statute of the International Court of Justice.

4. As it is called in the common law systems.

5. As it is called in civil law systems.

6. This is easier said than done. But the idea, here, is to open up the possibility for bringing in the institutional practice closer to private sector practices, at least when an operation involves private partners.

7. In this context, it may be useful to note that following the approval by the World Bank's Executive Directors in 2012 of the "Proposed Adoption and Application of World Bank Performance Standards for Private Sector Projects Supported by IBRD/IDA" (June 26, 2012; R2012-0130; IDA/R2012-0161) of the use by the World Bank of IFC's Performance Standards. Also, the Bank has adopted OP/ BP 4.03, "Performance Standards for Private Sector Activities," which may be applied in lieu of the World Bank's safeguards under OP 4.01, for certain private sector activities supported by the World Bank. See also generally, IFC's Sustainability Framework, From Policy to Implementation (IFC December 2012). See also box 6.1 in chapter 6. See also, for some reference, Modernizing the Delivery of Complex Transformational Regional (Infrastructure) Project in Africa, First Discussion Draft, Regional Integration Department (March 1, 2013), 8.

8. Interestingly, there is increased corporate attention within the World Bank group on better risk management on Projects, which has led recently to the appointment of a Chief Risk Officer.

9. See also generally, Modernizing the Delivery of Complex Transformational Regional (Infrastructure) Project in Africa, First Discussion Draft, Regional Integration Department (March 1, 2013), 5.

10. See also generally, Modernizing the Delivery of Complex Transformational Regional (Infrastructure) Project in Africa, First Discussion Draft, Regional Integration Department (March 1, 2013), 18, suggesting more creative and strategic division of labor among development partners. This could also, as a consequence, potentially generate changes in the framework arrangements between the Bank and development partners.

11. See Ryan T. Ketchum, "Cooperation Amid Conflict," *Handshake, IFC's Quarterly Journal on Public*-Private Partnership, Theme on Reconstruction PPPs (April 2013), 63.

12. Implemented first at the European Union, the concept of structural funds is based on the premise of making several sources of money available to member states to encourage economic development and to bring all members to roughly the same stage of advancement. Funds are intended to facilitate structural adjustment of specific sectors, regions, or combinations of both. The European Regional Development Fund, the European Social Fund, and the European Agricultural Guidance and Guarantee Fund are some of the examples.

13. In that vein, World Bank and SAARC secretariat signed a "cooperation arrangement" in 2002. In that same year, the World Bank had also planned to provide some grant funds for SAARC's capacity development (through its Institutional Development Fund grant window), but due to a number of difficult policy-related reasons, and after several months of discussions, the grant never materialized.

CHAPTER 8

Conclusion

The foregoing chapters have shown that, although a general pattern applicable to most of them may be discerned, regional projects in various continents are still being designed and finalized in different ways. If some have been designed in the context of a relatively well-developed legal framework, others have had to fit in an environment completely lacking in it; if some are put forward in a politically homogenous environment, others have had to deal with total heterogeneity;[1] and if some have narrowly focused on a defined sector, others have taken a multisector or an integrated approach.[2]

It is clear, therefore, that in view of the unique situation each continent, region, and operation may present, the best practice for the World Bank, first and foremost, should be a detailed and serious due diligence work, before making any decision pertaining to the legal model for a regional operation. The due diligence work should be able to make an assessment of all concerned private or public sector partners, collect ample data for the Bank to design the project in such a way that risks are minimized and opportunity costs are reduced, and are also able to improve the situation of countries, beneficiaries, and the goal of development *per se*.

Each specific circumstance will dictate legal solutions. Therefore, a gradation of legal instruments in this study may not be wise. If in some situations it may be necessary to have a treaty ratified upfront, then in some others, the ratification may be staggered, and in others, instead of a treaty, soft instruments may be advisable. If in some situations private sector lead may be more efficient, thus letting market to decide on many of the issues, and create indirect leveraging mechanisms, then in others, public sector lead may be advantageous. Similarly, if in some situations multifaceted interventions may be useful, then in others, more narrow and focused interventions may be appropriate. Also if in some situations it may be wise to clarify all the roles and responsibilities and decision making upfront, then in others, it may be better to devise a mechanism to ensure that decision making will rely on a dynamic system suitable for the project, an in-built flexible mechanism, which will allow continual and ongoing adaptability to decision making.

This exercise of finding legal solution should, however, include some level of short-term trendcasting based on extrapolation from recent practice; some level of normative arguments for legal or institutional changes framed with reference to different alternatives and eventualities; and some preparation of contingency lists (listing alternative paths and contexts for legal architecture, along with assessments of relative likelihood of different scenarios).

It is important to bear in mind that the current global environment provides a historically unprecedented scale of capital flows, trade opportunities, information, and technologies, which, if utilized, can dramatically transform the material and social conditions of life of people everywhere, and more so in Asia. But this vision would be efficacious only to the extent that it can be concretized. This concretization requires bringing to bear a new consciousness in the region, a new development pattern, not state-centric, but region-centric. Indeed, it may be beneficial for the region to develop and implement regional projects that take a holistic approach toward the collective good of the region. Some scholars have noted, "Regional cooperation begets economic wealth. Economic wealth begets strength."[3] By adding a new modality in their development wheel, supported by various legal tools and instruments, the Asian countries can collaborate regionally for, among other, managing transboundary problems and exploring the possibilities for building a partnership for development in selected sectors.

There is little doubt that, like all regions, Asia holds the potential within its borders to overcome its many problems. But this potential should be transformed into tangible outcomes, which could be possible by considering, designing, and implementing regional projects and designing even more adaptable legal instruments[4] to be used in different situations, scenarios, and settings, and that too, with certain amount of consistency. Indeed, as noted by the president of the World Bank, Dr. Jim Yong Kim, "the hallmark of delivery excellence is consistency."[5]

Notes

1. The heterogeneous legal environment can often be a source of legal complexity and even uncertainty, and can have significant consequences for all public and private sector entities involved in cross-border initiatives. One way to minimize that complexity is by tackling the "cross-border effects" by pooling funds, knowledge, and competencies, initiating formal cross-border cooperation, leading to joint definition of strategic priorities for the future of the cross-border areas, and establishing joint cross-border management structures.

2. One point of caution may be warranted. The examples provided in the previous sections have not all necessarily been successful. For example, the CASAREM or the GMSREM have been delayed, many are still being implemented (with varying levels of difficulty), and the results and outcomes of other projects that were completed have not yet been evaluated. Interestingly, this situation also strengthens the argument that the commitment and ownership (discussed in chapter 3) need to be secured upfront

3. Lorraine C. Cardenas and Arpaporn Buranakanits, "The Role of APEC in the Achievement of Regional Cooperation in Southeast Asia," *Annual Survey of International & Comparative Law* 5, 1, 80.

4. Not that the IDOs do not have adaptable instruments already, but the idea is that there should be more of these instruments, which further need to be publicized.

5. "Toward a Global Science of Delivery," The Art and Science of Delivery, In honor of the 10th anniversary of the Skoll World Forum (McKinsey & Co, 2013), 53.

Selected References

Ahmed, Sadiq, Saman Kalegama, and Ejaz Ghani, eds. 2010. *Promoting Economic Cooperation in South Asia: Beyond SAFTA*. World Bank/Sage Publications.

Al Habsy, Said N., and Kishor Uprety. 2010. *Sustaining Development and Peace South Asian Association for Regional Cooperation. International, Institutional and Legal Perspectives*. University Press Limited.

Anghie, Antony. 2012. "Identifying Regions In the History of International Law." In *The History of International Law*, edited by Bardo Fassbender and Anne Peters (Simone Peter and Daniel Hogger, Asst. Eds.). Oxford University Press.

Bhattacharya, Biswa Nath. 2010. "Estimating Demand for Infrastructure." Energy, Transport, Telecommunications, Water and Sanitation in Asia and the Pacific: 2010–2020, ADBI Working Paper Series, No. 248, September.

Cardenas, Lorraine C., and Arpaporn Buranakanits. 1999. "The Role of APEC in the Achievement of Regional Cooperation in Southeast Asia."*Annual Survey Of International & Comparative Law* 5 (1).

Detlef, Lorenz. 1991. "Regionalisation versus Regionalism—Problems of Change in the World Economy." *Intereconomics* (January/February).

De, Prabir. 2011. "Why is Trade at Borders a Costly Affair in South Asia? An Empirical Investigation."*Contemporary South Asia* 19 (4): 441–64. Routledge.

Devlin, Robert, and Lucio Castro. 2002. "Regional Banks and Regionalism: A New Frontier for Development Financing." Paper Prepared for a Conference "On Financing for Development: Regional Challenges & the Regional Development Banks" at The Institute for International Economics.

Guidelines for Accessing IDA Regional Funding, World Bank.

IDA 14 Mid-Term Review of the IDA Pilot Program for Regional Projects IDA 14, International Development Association Regional Integration Department, Africa Region, November 2006.

Kessides, Ioannis N., Roger G. Noll, and Nancy C. Benjamin. Publication Date Unknown. *Regionalizing Infrastructure Reform in Developing Countries*. World Bank.

Lawson, Ruth C. 1962. *International Regional Organizations. Constitutional Foundations*. New York: Praeger.

Malla, Shanker Krishna. 2008. "Towards a Regional Energy Market in South Asia." SACEPS Paper No. 16, May.

Ollila, Petri, Juha I. Uitto, Christophe Crepin, and Alfred M. Duda. 2000. "Multicountry Project Arrangements. Report of a Thematic Review." World Bank, September.

Prabhu, Suresh P. 2012. "India's Water Challenges." Atlantic Council Issue Brief, October.

Pyakuryal, Bishwambher, and Kishor Uprety. 2005. "Economic & Legal Impact of Conflict on States & People in South Asia with Specific Reference to Nepal." *Journal Of Social, Political And Economic Studies* 30 (4): 459–95.

Rapley, John. 2008. *Understanding Development: Theory and Practice in the Third World.* 3rd ed. Boulder and London: Lynne Rienner.

Regional Operations Toolkit, A Resource Guide to Facilitate Design, Processing, & Implementation of Regional Projects in Africa, December 2009.

"Regional Energy Projects: Experience & Approaches of the World Bank Group." Background Paper for the World Bank Group Energy Strategy, February 2010.

Romdhane, Saoussen Ben, and Emanuele Santi. 2012. "Defining Regional Integration: Key Concepts & Theories." In *Unlocking North Africa's Potential through Regional Integration. Challenges & Opportunities,* edited by Emanuele Santi, Saoussen Ben Romdhane, and William Shaw. AfDB.

Strategic and Operational Framework for Regional Operations. African Development Bank Group, January 8, 2008.

Upadhyaya, Anup Kumar. "South Asia Regional Energy Cooperation: Opportunities & Challenges." Discussion paper, Economic Integration in South Asia, Nepal Rastra Bank.

UNIDO. 2012. "Executive Summary." Networks for Prosperity: Achieving Development Goals through Knowledge Sharing.

World Bank. 1995. "Cross-Border Initiative to Promote Private Investment, Trade and Payments in Eastern and Southern Africa & the Indian Ocean." May 15.

——. 2006. "The Development Potential of Regional Programs an Evaluation of World Bank Support of Multicountry Operations." Submitted to the Committee on Development Effectiveness Meeting, February 14, 2007. December 19.

——. 2011a. Africa's Future & The World Bank's Support to It. March.

——. 2011b. "Partnering for Africa's Regional Integration." Progress Report on the Regional Integration Assistance Strategy for Sub-Saharan Africa, World Bank, March.

——. 2011c. *World Development Report 2011: Conflict, Security, and Development.* Washington, DC: World Bank.

——. 2013. "Modernizing the Delivery of Complex Transformational Regional (Infrastructure) Project in Africa." First Discussion Draft, Regional Integration Department, World Bank, March 1.

World Bank Operations. 1972. *Sectoral Programs & Policies.* Baltimore and London: Johns Hopkins University Press.

Environmental Benefits Statement

The World Bank is committed to reducing its environmental footprint. In support of this commitment, the Publishing and Knowledge Division leverages electronic publishing options and print-on-demand technology, which is located in regional hubs worldwide. Together, these initiatives enable print runs to be lowered and shipping distances decreased, resulting in reduced paper consumption, chemical use, greenhouse gas emissions, and waste.

The Publishing and Knowledge Division follows the recommended standards for paper use set by the Green Press Initiative. Whenever possible, books are printed on 50 percent to 100 percent postconsumer recycled paper, and at least 50 percent of the fiber in our book paper is either unbleached or bleached using Totally Chlorine Free (TCF), Processed Chlorine Free (PCF), or Enhanced Elemental Chlorine Free (EECF) processes.

More information about the Bank's environmental philosophy can be found at http://crinfo.worldbank.org/wbcrinfo/node/4.